2/14/16

To: Jenna
We love you!

p~~~~~~~~~~ paul

D1055500

Especially For

*Jenna Carol*

From

*Nanna and Pepaul*

Date

*2/14/16*

# You're
# Late Again,
## Lord

# You're Late Again, Lord

## Journaling Your Way to a Patient Heart

Karon Phillips

BARBOUR BOOKS
An Imprint of Barbour Publishing, Inc.

Published by Barbour Books, an imprint of Barbour Publishing, Inc., P.O. Box 719, Uhrichsville, Ohio 44683, www.barbourbooks.com

*Our mission is to publish and distribute inspirational products offering exceptional value and biblical encouragement to the masses.*

Member of the
Evangelical Christian
Publishers Association

Printed in China.

# Dedication

*To my mother, who always believed in me,
even when reason or circumstance said she shouldn't.*

# Contents

# Introduction

*I wait for the LORD, my soul waits,*
*And in His word I do hope.*
PSALM 130:5 NKJV

I have to be, without a doubt, one of the most impatient people our Lord ever put on this earth. Perhaps you're a close second, or Heaven forbid, even worse. We live, therefore, we wait. It seems endless. Forever we wait on something to happen in our lives—to get a job or to get a promotion, to quit a job or to move, to sell a house or to buy a house, to save money or to have children, to start school or to finish school, to get through a difficult time or to overcome a hurt— it's always something. Whoever said "life is short" must have never known the frustration of waiting forever on something that never seems to come.

Sometimes, our days feel like one long checkout line: constantly waiting, barely inching forward, unable to see the obstacles, doubtful of a satisfactory outcome in this lifetime. And then what we're waiting for comes or it doesn't, we adjust, recover and move on. But are we any better for the wait? Did we find the purpose the Lord had tucked so carefully inside? Did we listen to God and learn, or did we just complain about the circumstances?

Either way, when that wait is over, we shift our focus to a new wait, and the feelings are all very familiar. Again, we grow impatient. The cycle never ends. Through all the delays that we misunderstand, we never seem to get very far from where we started. We stand still on the path that matters most. The waiting is nothing more than a time of frustration. We argue with our Lord over His timing and fail to see that every day is a chance, full of purpose—even if we're waiting. "Many are the plans in a person's heart, but it is the LORD's purpose that prevails" (Proverbs 19:21 NIV).

Yet we resist, complain, and sometimes get quite angry. Desperate for God's touch, we move farther from Him when we should be moving closer. Do you ever find yourself in that kind of cycle—angry, frustrated, and anything but patient for God?

If you do, welcome to the club, the *Impatient Women's Club*. Our numbers swell daily when we are forced to abandon our normal plan of attack and wait on God. We have become so accustomed to ordering and orchestrating and planning and scheduling that it is incredibly hard to admit that not all is within our control. Many decisions every day are ours to handle, and we get pretty good at taking care of things. We believe that we could carry on even better if God would only cooperate. We demand the answers we need from Him, and yet we hear no response. We question and condemn the intolerable delays in the events we need to happen in our lives, and yet nothing changes. Doesn't God know that we need those answers *now?*

Yes, He knows, but thankfully, He's smarter than we are. Because He knows how hard it is for us to wait, to abandon control, and to trust beyond ourselves, He has devised a plan just for us. The basis of the plan appeared many years ago, but it applies so well today, to you and me. God is so clever. Your waiting doesn't have to be unproductive—He knows our workhorse hearts. He knows our need to do *while* we wait. So when your life is at a standstill over what you can't control, and when you're waiting on answers that never seem to come, God says to use that time to work where you are. God says to learn *the art of waiting purposefully.* Maybe that's what God had in mind all along. Maybe that's why we wait.

Our stubborn hearts resist the wait, yet there is no need. "Therefore, my beloved brethren, be steadfast, immovable, always abounding in the work of the Lord, knowing that your labor is not in vain in the Lord" (1 Corinthians 15:58 NKJV). We do steadfast and immovable pretty well, don't you think? In this case, the instruction is to "stand firm" and not be swayed from God's work. The instruction is to follow God instead of trying so very hard to hurry Him up.

When we ignore God's work for us, we misuse our valuable time and yet can't understand why we have to wait over and over and over again. You know the feeling. You see the waiting as an inconvenience, but instead, it is a gift. There is no better time than waiting time to learn how to become the disciple God needs and the follower you want to be. Your work during that time is the vehicle that will get you closer to God, if you let it. The Lord, in His generosity and compassion, has already provided everything you need. You can uncover the amazing blessings the waiting brings.

Beware, though, because the plan God has provided takes work. It's no quick fix. *Waiting purposefully* means working while you wait, following God's Word and surrendering to His will. It means focusing on *His* view, not *yours*. It means coming face-to-face with God, in all His glory and all your humility. It rarely means waiting for what you *think* you're waiting for, but don't ever be afraid: the reward is worth the work, and you don't have to wait. You can start now.

## PART 1

# The Highly Overrated Virtue of Patience

*But those who wait on the Lord*
*shall renew their strength;*
*They shall mount up with wings like eagles,*
*They shall run and not be weary,*
*They shall walk and not faint.*

Isaiah 40:31 NKJV

Chapter 1—*He Has a Plan*

I wish I had a nickel for every time I've asked the Lord for patience. All I'd have to wait for then would be the latest tally of my money. Of all the countless times I've asked God for patience, I've never gotten it, not even once. Maybe He just grew tired of listening to my same request over and over. Finally, one day God and I had a serious talk. I used to think that I started it, but I've come to realize that He did.

"I can't stand this, Lord. I am always waiting, for this or that, and it's all important. I simply can't stand it anymore. You've got to do something," I prayed and protested aloud. I was desperate. My strength and my spirit were suffering.

"No, you've got to do something. I pointed it out so plainly so many years ago, but you just keep ignoring it," God said. "That's why we keep coming back here."

"Sorry...," I replied.

God and I had been at this juncture many times before. I was trying to learn what He wanted to teach, but I was as stubborn as I was frustrated. Sometimes I wonder where God found the patience to deal with me.

There is no question that we live our lives according to God's timing. After all, it's His world and only He knows how to make the clock work. "To everything there is a season, A time for every purpose under heaven" (Ecclesiastes 3:1 NKJV). Still, we want to be in charge.

The world, though, revolves around His timing, not mine or yours. You wouldn't think His omnipotent control of time would come as such a revelation, but the got-it-together, always-prepared, on-top-of-things woman that I'd always been, refused for many years to believe that I couldn't eliminate the waiting in my life with enough determination and persistence. All of that effort was sorely misplaced, I can see now. My thoughts seemed to make sense to me all that time, but God knew their weaknesses.

Waiting is inevitable for us all. We can either spend the time with complaints and arguments and disgust or use the time for worship and growth and understanding. God said so. The plan He devised long ago gives us a goal and the tools to reach it. "Those who wait on the LORD shall renew their strength" (Isaiah 40:31 NKJV). Nothing zaps your strength and energy and feeling of purpose like having to wait. When we have to wait, we feel powerless and abandoned. But we can renew our strength when we wait on the Lord. And that was certainly what I needed: my strength and spirit renewed, refreshed, and reborn.

In many interpretations of God's message, the words "wait" and "hope" are used interchangeably. That makes sense. Waiting is always filled with hope. Hope implies something yet to come. And both reveal complete dependence on the Lord. "Wait and hope in me," He says, "and while you're there, do these things. . . ."

He doesn't say wait and hope and sit quietly. He says to *mount up*, to *run*, and to *walk*—these are words that indicate anything but inaction. These words require *work*. These words come with a purpose. You can fulfill the Lord's purpose for you *while* you wait and hope. What a plan. I told you He was smart.

> *Does he who fashioned the ear not hear?*
> *Does he who formed the eye not see?*
> *Does he who disciplines nations not punish?*
> *Does he who teaches mankind lack knowledge?*
> *The Lord knows all human plans;*
> *he knows that they are futile.*
> PSALM 94:9–11 NIV

We can't hurry God, and we can't bribe Him or force Him to alter the plan He's made. But we can learn to trust Him not to waste our waiting time—He's far too economical for that. He knows our shortcomings and yet, He still reaches for us, over and over again, even when we resist. Our job, always, is to cooperate, to listen, to learn, and our goal is to accomplish God's work for us—*in His time.*

Knowing our human, shortsighted demands for reason and action, He prepared the guideline for us long ago. He reminded me of it that day when I was complaining without end, when I questioned His care and concern and wondered if He was just going to abandon me forever. Considering how often I thought I didn't need His help, He probably wanted to now and then.

"Can't You see how needy I am for Your answers?" I begged again.

"Why can't you remember the guidance I gave you all those years ago?" He countered.

"Because my head's as dense as a fence post?" I offered.

"I was going to say because you won't slow down and focus on me. You want to reach for the answers before you ask the right questions. You fail to ask for what you need the most."

"What do I need the most?"

"You need *me*. You need to feel me beside you and know that that's enough for whatever lies ahead, instead of trying to harness me into your schedule. You need to renew your spirit first and continually. Slow down, and let me help you."

"I'll do my best, but You know how I am. . . ."

"That's okay, we'll work it out. Just please pay attention this time, and let's review again," He said.

"I'm ready," I told Him.

## Remembering

I listened more closely that time God spoke, whether out of desperation or exasperation, I don't know. I recalled that first day He had tried to get through to me with His plan, His peace.

In what feels like a thousand years ago, fresh out of college, I was a reporter for a small daily newspaper. I covered the police calls and fire alarms, city council meetings, and planning commission rezonings. And every four weeks, the rotation for the "church feature" fell to me. That meant that I had to write an interesting story with a spiritual slant for that weekend's paper. One week, I interviewed a young man who had built a great program for the youth at his church. He was preparing to leave for college where he would study to become a minister. He was a fascinating person, and our conversation led to his search for the right university.

He said he was looking for guidance from God on which school to attend. He believed that he found it at the last campus he visited, where the Bible verse on the sign out front was Isaiah 40:31, his favorite.

He quoted it to me beautifully, and I can still hear him today, even though I've long since forgotten his name or the school he chose. And though my memory fails miserably on every other occasion, I have heard that verse go flawlessly through my mind ever since. I don't know that I had ever heard it before, but as soon as I did, I felt like it was mine, all mine.

> *But those who wait on the*
> *LORD shall renew their strength;*
> *They shall mount up with wings like eagles,*
> *They shall run and not be weary,*
> *They shall walk and not faint.*
> ISAIAH 40:31 NKJV

Even though I loved the beauty and simplicity in those words and craved their comfort, I would still fight God for control every time I had to slow my life down and wait. I would console myself with those words, and then in the same breath, plead again for the answers I had already determined to be the right ones. I was too busy talking to listen, but God was never too busy for me. "Are not two sparrows sold for a copper coin? And not one of them falls to the ground apart from your Father's will. But the very hairs on your head are all numbered. Do not fear therefore; you are of more value than many sparrows" (Matthew 10:29–31 NKJV).

"That means you, too, you know," He said.

"Even while I wait?"

"Especially while you wait."

## ❖ While You Wait ❖

‐   How do you react when you have to wait for something?

‐   How does your spirit and strength suffer when you're waiting?

‐   Think about how you want to *mount up*, *run*, and *walk* into a closer relationship with God.

............................................................................................

............................................................................................

............................................................................................

............................................................................................

............................................................................................

............................................................................................

............................................................................................

............................................................................................

............................................................................................

............................................................................................

............................................................................................

............................................................................................

............................................................................................

............................................................................................

............................................................................................

............................................................................................

# CHAPTER 2—He Talks to Me

~~~~~~~~~~~~

As God and I had our talk that day, I felt empty and alone. I had been waiting for so long, trying to be as patient as I knew how and looking for reasons in my delays. I felt powerless: I couldn't do anything to change my life, and God *wouldn't* do anything to change it. Of course, I was wrong (again). God would do anything I needed, but I had to know how to ask and how to listen. I had to know how to wait and hope in Him, to go to Him *first*, not last.

"Whoever belongs to God hears what God says. The reason you do not hear is that you do not belong to God" (John 8:47 NIV). I couldn't hear anything over my own demands. I didn't have time to belong to God—I wanted *Him* to belong to *me*. I know, it sounds ridiculous, but perhaps you've had the same feelings when you've felt oppressed by a wait. I had created my own abandonment in the "waiting room" God had created for my growth.

Was it not *me* who complained endlessly about God while failing to see where I needed to make some changes of my own? Was it not *me* who demanded that heaven and earth operate on my timetable, as if I were in charge and could order God Himself around? Was it not *me* who stood in the way of what I so desperately wanted: understanding and answers, a kinship with God that did not falter? My goodness! My bullheadedness must have tried God's patience on more than one occasion! Forever the Comforter, though, "The LORD is merciful and gracious, Slow to anger, and abounding in mercy" (Psalm 103:8 NKJV).

I wonder how many times He was amused at my ranting, my fruitless, egotistical ravings for action *now!* Still, there He was, when

I asked—*again*—explaining my work to me, again trying to help me see what was so plainly there. The lesson was about waiting, all right, but waiting with a *purpose*. "Wait on me and you shall mount up and run and walk," He said, but in my haste and misguided efforts, I only tripped.

I wanted answers, no strings attached. God said, "Okay, you'll get your answers, but I need you to work while you wait for them and to ask the right questions."

"Not good enough," I said. I was willing to listen as long as God would say what I wanted to hear. When He wouldn't, I'd complain more about nothing happening all the while God was giving me the opportunity to make *plenty* happen—to make the most *important* thing happen, which was growing toward Him, and yet I resisted.

My preoccupation with the wait in my life overshadowed my own needs and weaknesses that I couldn't see. I believe that God thought it was time I finally addressed them because He knew how they were destroying me from within. My frustration with the waiting time was only the outward sign. He provided the opportunity to grow closer to Him within the wait that I detested so.

If the Lord thought that I was finally ready to listen and learn, He was right. If necessity is the mother of invention, then desperation is surely the mother of decision. I made my choice that day. I was ready to learn those lessons He had for me, to learn *the art of waiting purposefully*, of working on His timeline. I had no idea how long the lessons would take. The fact is that they continue today, and I accept.

*My soul longs for You like a thirsty land.*
PSALM 143:6 NKJV

## Teach me

I was ready to learn, but I didn't know how. I didn't have a clue where to start, but the work was becoming clearer.

"See, there is plenty for you to do while you wait, *especially* you," God said.

No need to get personal. . . .

For years, I believed that proper faith had to mean doing nothing but waiting patiently on the Lord, without action or question. And I doubted my faith because I wasn't very good at sitting patiently and waiting quietly. What I had seen as a failure of *faith* was in fact a failure of *purpose*.

"Aren't I just supposed to wait without question? Isn't that the way to faith?" I had asked.

"No, proper faith means waiting purposefully with me as my plan unfolds, trusting in *me*," He said. "I'll show you how if you will only see. Time is valuable, and you're misusing it with your endless attempts to control it. You don't need to do that—you need to fill it with something much more useful than your complaints about how its passing suits your schedule."

Wow, He had me pegged on that one.

"So You've got a plan for me, but still I must wait?"

"Yes, sometimes, you must wait for me, but with a *purposeful* patience. Your impatience can't change my plan anyway. It's your work I'm interested in. There is much to do."

I had always wanted so much to get to the "doing" part quickly—*my* way: I would try to reason with God and get Him to understand my logic and grasp of the situation. It's laughable now, how I always had it all figured out and thought that He was always late. I had done all of the work for Him—arranged everything, answered the questions—all He had to do was follow my lead, and yet He refused. I often skipped the part about asking what *He* wanted. And I neglected the part about what *I* needed. Now I know that God doesn't neglect any part, and all of my work without Him is useless.

"There is no wisdom, no insight, no plan that can succeed against the Lord" (Proverbs 21:30 NIV). And there is no plan that the Lord has for me that isn't what I need or won't get me where I need to be. (You'd think I would have gotten that sooner. . . .) I always wanted to complete the waiting, and I cared little about what benefits were in it for me. I could not see any delay as a positive development, so of course, I could never learn the lessons. I just thought I had failed because I couldn't be the quiet and patient disciple I once thought I had to be. God showed me another way.

God showed me the part of the plan I had always ignored, that moving closer to Him was the journey I could embark on today, not a destination too far away to see.

Waiting on God's answers doesn't mean silent resignation to empty days or weeks or even months or years. It means working purposefully as I await the next development in His plan. I don't need a copy of the blueprints. I can work while I wait.

"Okay," I told Him. "I think I understand."

I could see God sitting there, winded and forever patient. He sighs heavily, a little skeptical but hopeful. I've failed so many times before.

"Perhaps it isn't patience I need, then, but purpose? Then through the wait, my spirit is renewed. With new strength and purpose, I can help us both. I can use the waiting time that has always destroyed me in the past, and I can do the work You have for me. Nothing is wasted."

"Not bad," He said. "Now, let's go with that. You don't have to wait *patiently* when you learn to wait *purposefully*. When would you like to start?"

*Show me Your ways, O LORD;*
*Teach me Your paths.*
*Lead me in Your truth and teach me,*
*For You are the God of my salvation;*
*On You I wait all the day.*
PSALM 25:4–5 NKJV

## ⸙ *While You Wait* ⸙

– What do you think God is trying to tell you when you have to wait?

– How can you listen more effectively for His instruction?

– Think about the kind of disciple you want to become while you wait.

# CHAPTER 3—A Light Bulb Came On!

Wow, I liked the way this was going! I had finally heard God tell me that I didn't have to be patient at all—I just had to be purposeful. And in His infinite wisdom, He had already provided all that I needed: "And God is able to make all grace abound to you, so that in all things at all times, having all that you need, you will abound in every good work" (2 Corinthians 9:8 NIV). Of course! Those words are about giving, it's true, but they are about other kinds of work, too. And the Lord says that *at all times*, I will have what I need so that I can abound in *every good work*. All of those times include waiting times, too. Maybe He wasn't really late after all. . . .

The time I spent waiting didn't have to be endless and useless—it could be productive and dynamic. Living according to my Lord's timetable included my work, too. I could be both prayerful and purposeful. I could "pray without ceasing" while I worked. I could listen and learn. God had prepared for my impatience. He had provided a place for me to grow. He was going to be there while we waited to help me find what I had lost, and He and I both knew that was a long list.

It's been too many years to remember when I ever felt bored, but when I hear someone say that today, I stand in amazement. Waiting for one thing may keep me from doing what I had planned, but there is never enough waiting time to be bored. My goodness, the things there are to work on! "Therefore we do not lose heart. Though outwardly we are wasting away, yet inwardly we are being renewed day by day" (2 Corinthians 4:16 NIV). The renewal of my spirit is a never-ending joyride, and God is there day by day, *every* day.

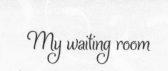

# My waiting room

I had always equated waiting with standing still, the time a useless, inconvenient intrusion into my busy life. I was wrong. The waiting time did not exist in a vacuum. The time came packed with opportunities and discoveries, but I had to do the work to find them. I like to work. God had finally gotten through to me with that message—I can work while I wait, and there is never a shortage of worthy projects.

"You are finally beginning to recognize your waiting room, aren't you?" He asked.

"I think so. My waiting room is mine alone, and for very special reasons. Please forgive my complaints in the past—I didn't know. Now I understand. I'm here so that I can rediscover what I've lost and learn more about what I need to do. I'm here so that I can renew my strength and my spirit. We both know that I couldn't have gone on much longer like this. I'm here so that I can move, *closer to You.*"

God and I just sat there for a while after that revelation. It was one of those "smack yourself in the forehead" moments, and finally, I had slowed down long enough for it to happen. God, infinitely wise and patient, had even prepared for His children like me. Was there no end to His wisdom and compassion? Was there no end to what He could teach me?

"For with God nothing will be impossible," the angel Gabriel said (Luke 1:37 NKJV). I'll trust that to mean even *me:* that God could teach even *me* how to wait purposefully, to learn along the way, to do the work He has for me. He certainly likes to challenge Himself, though, I'll give Him that, and yet He has never failed me. "For I, the LORD your God, will hold your right hand, Saying to you, 'Fear not, I will help you'" (Isaiah 41:13 NKJV).

God had put me again and again in my waiting room, not to frustrate me or frighten me, but to *teach* and *reach* me. I was fighting to get out ahead of schedule, which was pointless, when I should have been learning how to wait.

He sighed heavily again.

"I'm glad you've finally begun to see this. I know that slowing down and listening first goes against your nature. . . ," He began.

"You made me, remember?" (I thought I'd slip that one in there just for me.)

"Yes, but you have poorly used the valuable time I've given you, drifted away from me, and lost sight of your work. Understand?"

Of course, I knew it'd be my fault.

"Let's start with a little work up front on that control issue of yours," He said.

I knew this was going to be bad.

## ✦ While You Wait ✦

- Talk to God about why you're in your waiting room right now.

- How will you let Him help you renew your strength and your spirit, beginning today?

.......................................................................................
.......................................................................................
.......................................................................................

# Chapter 4—*Looking Inside*

Those of you who, like me, tend to be a little impatient now and then, probably also tend to be just a little on the controlling side. That's fine if you're potty training a Great Dane, but you can't wait purposefully and control the rest of the world at the same time. Believe me, I've tried. And God, in His unfathomable patience, has waited on me through each pointless, misguided effort, and there have been plenty.

Ever since I was a little girl, I thought that if I could just stay a step ahead of everyone else, neatly package and prepare everything, there would be no unpleasant surprises to impact my timetable. Forever compulsive, I would plan ahead for every event, anticipate problems, seek remedies, devise contingency plans, and pretty much organize my world around my schedule. I know, there's nothing wrong with a little forethought, but I made a SWAT team look slow to react. In all of that struggle for control, I failed to see what I could gain by giving up that control to God.

The Lord let me go on like this for many years, pretty much through high school, college, and well into my thirties (talk about patient). Again, it's not wrong to be prepared, but such compulsion can lead you to a feeling of control that isn't yours. When you look to yourself for all the answers and explanations and guidelines, it will make you doubt everything—ultimately including yourself—because you will fail miserably. When you're trying to hold on to the control that you *think* you have, you never see what God is trying to help you rediscover.

*Therefore humble yourselves*
*under the mighty hand of God,*

*that He may exalt you in due time,*
*casting all your care upon Him,*
*for He cares for you.*
1 PETER 5:6–7 NKJV

I looked only to myself, and I failed. I never learned what my waiting room experience was there to teach me. All the while, the "mighty hand of God" was there, but, for reasons that make sense only to us control freaks, I wanted to handle my cares alone. I felt that I knew better than God what was best for me, or at least which path was the most convenient. Still, it didn't matter. As much as I protested and complained and argued, it was all a matter of God's "due time." I was fighting the wrong battle. God knew the right one.

Waiting isn't about what happens *outside* you—it's about what happens *inside* you.

Always, always, when you wait, no matter what you *think* you're waiting for, you—and God—are always waiting on changes and discoveries inside yourself. God needs those changes and discoveries before you can do the next job He has for you. He has a plan, a blessed syllabus for your life, and it's always charted from the inside out.

When your wait is over, the outward one that you can see, it's because you've accomplished the work that God had for you to do inside yourself *during that wait*, and you and He together will know when that happens. You'll feel the change as you rediscover the strength you had lost, and it will match your need at the time. So don't be afraid to look for what you need. It's already there, and the Lord says, "Come closer, closer. . ."

Remember that you are never waiting for the things the world will see—those are just the temporary developments so that God can get your full attention. Your internal work is far more important than any external change. You can't get where God wants you to be and claim control at the same time, though. It's not possible.

"I control this wait and all the others. You know that, don't you?" God asks.

"Yes, but I want so much to handle it on my own."

"Why? Don't you also know that that's what I'm here for? My part is the easy part. You make your part harder when you won't allow me to help you."

"Others make it look easy. . . ," I point out.

"What others? There is only you and me in this wait. I can see I have a little more explaining to do."

Uh-oh.

## ⋟ *While You Wait* ⋞

‒ Where in your life and your wait do you need to relinquish control?

‒ How have you let your need for control separate you from God?

‒ How have you neglected internal changes that God needs from you by trying to control external changes you can see?

# Chapter 5— *The Comparison Trap*

While you're trying to control your whole world, you can sometimes fall into the Comparison Trap, too. If you're caught by this snare, you compare your progress or loss, your circumstances and events—*your wait*—to mine and everyone else's. It's a terrible waste of your time and resources. That's never what your wait is for.

Compare yourself only to *time*, not other people. Compare yourself before and after your stay in the waiting room. Are you closer to your Lord or farther away? Have the old attitudes and beliefs that fueled your need to control grown or diminished? Have you heard God speak to you more or less? I sound like the eye doctor, don't I? Well, maybe that fits, because it's all about your vision—learning to look *inside* instead of *out*, because God said that the outside didn't matter, that there were no "others."

"Your wait is not a contest," He said. "Your wait is with *me* alone."

It's quite simple: each wait should get us closer to God. Each wait should help us grow, if only a little bit, so that we can see ourselves and God better. Each stay in our waiting room should prepare and guide us for the work God has for us to do, without regard to what others are doing with their waits. "So is my word that goes out from my mouth: It will not return to me empty, but will accomplish what I desire and achieve the purpose for which I sent it" (Isaiah 55:11 NIV).

The trap is so easy to fall into because we let ourselves reach to others for what we need when God has already given it to us. It's like jumping out of a plane and reaching for someone else's parachute while mine sits idly on my back—I'd be doomed, and all because I couldn't see how to help myself with what was already provided especially for me.

In God's timing, everything is manifested when He chooses to make it so. Your part in His plan is based on the growth and the progress and the amazing revelations in your heart that happen regardless of what happens to me. What appears to be success or failure for me may, in fact, be God's instruction to me that you cannot understand. So compare yourself to no one. The only comparison that matters is God's, when He looks at you at the end of your wait and says, "Yes, you've grown, you've moved closer to me, you've weathered your wait and discovered my purpose. Now we can move on to even more wonderful glories." That's all that matters.

To learn the importance—and amazing peace—of only God's comparisons, surrender to God's timing. It is stunningly accurate. Surrendering to it is the only way to wait purposefully.

*But I trust in you, LORD;*
*I say, "You are my God."*
*My times are in your hands.*
PSALM 31:14–15 NIV

## ❧ While You Wait ❧

- How have you fallen into the Comparison Trap?

- Make a list of at least five comparisons that you need to let go of today.

- How will you let God help you out of the Comparison Trap?

# CHAPTER 6—Surrendering the Control

I used to *think* that I had surrendered to God now and then, but time would always tell that I really hadn't. I would just enjoy His company during some temporary unpleasantness in my life and then go back to doing everything my way. When God started to change my perspective and teach me how to wait purposefully, He had His work cut out for Him. He gave me example after example of His unlimited power and wisdom and invited me to follow. I, forever competent to run my own life (in my mind, at least), would retain what I'd learned for about, oh, two days, and then I would go back to controlling everything myself. Ha.

It was a long battle that the Lord waged with my will. I would convince myself from time to time that finally, one day God would surely decide that it was easier to just come around to my way of thinking, that He would adjust His timing to meet mine. I would pray to Him only to show Him the logic of doing things on my schedule, and then I'd sit and wait quite impatiently for it to happen. I wonder what He did while I was doing that? I imagine He just shook His head slowly and thought, *Maybe next time, she'll listen and surrender to me. . . .*

Listening is hard when we wait, especially if we're listening for the wrong things, for the Lord's surrender to *us* instead of our surrender to *Him*. One of the reasons we're often so hopelessly annoyed by the time we spend waiting is because the events are often completely out of our control. We're forced to sideline our plans until someone else completes His. What a pain. The frustration that inevitably follows causes us to seek even more control, and when we can't have it, we get even more frustrated. The result is wasted time, wasted energy, and another trip to the waiting room. Here we go again, fighting instead of surrendering, trusting ourselves more than God.

## The misunderstood comfort

I'm sure that my controlling nature was one of the main reasons that I couldn't hear God explaining this practice of surrender to me before, the surrender that says "my times are in Your hands. . . ." I bet you've felt that same way, haven't you, that you knew better than God? (Impatience breeds a little bit of arrogance now and then!) And when we feel that we know more than someone else does, it's almost impossible to submit to another's will. We fight it for so long because we are afraid of giving up the comfort that we believe comes from our control.

When we finally surrender into God's arms, the true comfort reaches down into our soul and steadies us from the inside out. It is both overpowering and liberating. "Not that we are sufficient of ourselves to think of anything as being from ourselves, but our sufficiency is from God" (2 Corinthians 3:5 NKJV). If we will allow it, God's sufficiency strengthens our spirit so that we need to control nothing except the work He has given us. That's all the control we need. It takes us a while to see it sometimes, but thankfully, God does patience a lot better than we do!

As much as I thought that I had learned every time God and I wrestled during a waiting time, it would still be many years before I would understand His call for purposeful waiting—for working on those things that I could and should control to get closer to Him. That's *my* job to accomplish with God's help. Waiting purposefully means remembering that God has been and always will be in complete control. That's *His* job.

*God is our refuge and strength, A very present help in trouble.*
*Therefore we will not fear, Even though the earth be removed,*
*And though the mountains be carried into the midst of the sea.*
PSALM 46:1–2 NKJV

I had learned, and forgotten, that truth many years before, and it helps me to recall it often, even now as I still fall back into old habits from time to time and allow my controlling nature to weasel its way back into my days. I'll tell you the story.

## ⸓ While You Wait ⸓

— In what wait has it been hardest for you to surrender control?

— If it's the wait you're in now, what first step can you take to surrender the control to God?

— How will you rely on God's sufficiency during your wait today?

................................................................................................................................

................................................................................................................................

................................................................................................................................

................................................................................................................................

................................................................................................................................

................................................................................................................................

................................................................................................................................

# Chapter 7—*God's Grace, My Ego*

Many years ago, on a cold, rainy February day, my family moved to a new town, a move we made because of my husband's job. We left behind a house and purchased another one in the new town. Our son was three.

I had decided that the move was wise, that it was okay for us to over-obligate ourselves financially, that our old house would sell very soon, that we could afford to continue to make payments on the property we'd recently bought, and that we would be happy in the new place. I had pretty much expected all of these things to happen because I wanted them to. They seemed logical enough, not a stretch for God's power, so why would He object? What lessons could possibly lay in that tiny bit of overstepped expectation?

I thought that those things I needed and wanted would be fairly unimportant to God, that perhaps He would supply them in part to end my constant nagging, and then He could move on to more important matters. Surely He didn't have the time to spend on me right then when I certainly didn't have the time to spend on Him.

Well, apparently, God *did* have the time, a whole year of it, in fact. My husband had a very rough time with his job that year. I struggled in my writing career. The house we'd left behind, about fifty long miles away, demanded weekly maintenance—two acres of grass to cut in the summer, aging pipes to protect in the winter. The strain on our marriage and our finances was overwhelming. I begged God for relief, because I couldn't control the mess no matter how hard I tried. I prayed for a buyer for the house. I prayed for help for my husband with his job. I prayed for deliverance while I cursed the wait and the worry. I didn't know what I was doing.

*"And which of you by worrying can add one cubit to your stature?
If you then are not able to do the least, why are you anxious for the rest?
But seek the kingdom of God, and all these things shall be added to you."*
LUKE 12:25–26, 31 NKJV

One day, the realtor called. There were problems with some kind of releases and transfers for the buyer he had finally found for our old house. The deal would probably fall through. I remember hanging up the phone and going to the bathroom. I propped myself over the sink and ran some water to pat on my swollen eyes. I couldn't hear a thing. I couldn't feel my breath. I stood there and looked in the mirror. It looked blank, but God was there. He's always there.

I don't know if I was praying or not, but I heard God say, "Don't worry, it'll be all right." It was an audible sound of words to my heart, to calm my worried mind. It was a brief breath of help, and I know why.

What I was waiting for wasn't the sale of the house or more money. It was reassurance that God was in control of my troubled world. "The righteous cry out, and the LORD hears them; he delivers them from all their troubles. The LORD is close to the brokenhearted and saves those who are crushed in spirit" (Psalm 34:17–18 NIV).

He was there. He renewed my strength and my spirit, and He let me mount up and run and walk when I thought there was nothing I could do. He showed me that there was, in fact, so very much that I could do. It wasn't what I expected, but it was what I needed, to look *inside* instead of out.

When I finally gave up that day, leaning against my bathroom counter, with nothing else to fight with, I turned to where I should have gone months before. I finally gave up trying to control the chaos of my life and, with a pure, surrendered heart, gave it to God. The relief was enormous.

# Waiting without fear

I could wait if I knew the Lord was there. I could wait with a purpose to work and draw nearer to Him, but I couldn't wait patiently while my whole life was falling apart. I think He knew that. I believe that my purpose for waiting that time was to develop the faith to turn to Him *first*, not *last*, to trust Him to always be there with me while I wait. The control I thought I had was never really there to begin with, but I had let the belief that it was blind me to the peace that God was offering with warm, outstretched arms. He knew when I could go no further alone. He knows if you're there, too. He always knows.

Just as Jesus knew when to stretch out His hand and keep Peter from sinking (Matthew 14:28–31), He knows when you are about to go under, when you are struggling with everything you face, and when you are so very afraid. "Immediately Jesus reached out his hand and caught him. 'You of little faith,' he said, 'why did you doubt?'" (Matthew 14:31 NIV).

We don't lose faith because we struggle. We struggle because we lose faith.

My very real problems didn't disappear that day, but I had made an important step. It was a few more months before our house sold, and the deal wasn't a lucrative one then, but it was a big relief. The land developer we had bought our land from wanted it back and we couldn't afford to keep it anyway, so we sold it and eliminated that payment. My husband's job situation improved somewhat and our marriage recovered for a time. I still cried endlessly on some days and ached with new pains when life hit hard and I was unprepared. I had dug myself into a pretty deep hole, and only God's grace could reach me. I would need it so often through the years, in even more frightful circumstances, and God would reach me then, too.

All of this work in my life took place in God's time and as part of His plan. I believe that His plan included that very day that I stood before my bathroom mirror and heard Him speak to my heart. It may sound selfish and egotistical to say that the Lord would use a year's worth of events to help one person grow a little faith, but I don't think so. It is in the times of waiting that we so desperately need to hold onto our faith, to uncover it when it's hidden by our egos, to know and believe that God is in control. Only when we believe that He is in control can we move our own need to control out of the way. Only then can we move on to the other work God has for us. Only then can we wait *purposefully*.

The lessons I learned during that time in my life were powerful, but afterward, when my life seemed to improve on the surface, I would slip and let the events of the day overshadow what God had taught me. I would run away when I thought I didn't need Him anymore, but He would always be there when I returned. The lessons never end, and He's always waiting for me. Still, today, I struggle with my overwhelming need to control. Still, God doesn't give up on me.

> *"I will not leave you as orphans;*
> *I will come to you."*
> JOHN 14:18 NIV

## ❧ While You Wait ❧

- Can you describe an experience in your life when you surrendered control to God, if only for a little while? How did it feel?

- How long did you hold onto God's peace then, and what made you let go of it?

# Chapter 8—*God Is in Control*

God has had to put me in my waiting room time and again, yet He never fails to help me out of it as well. When I'm there, and when I finally give up the control I'm seeking in such a futile way, I can see and believe again that He is in charge. He will tirelessly direct me in my quest for answers, the answers that lie only within my relationship with Him, the only ones that matter. I wait—for guidance, instruction, strength, and peace, to know my real purpose in this part of God's plan. But I don't have to wait patiently.

While God is handling the issues I *can't* begin to understand (like house sales and rejection letters), He is there to help me deal with the ones I *can* understand. There is in fact much that I can control if I choose to work while I wait, to work on those things God has put before me, to follow instead of fight.

> *"I am the vine, you are the branches.*
> *He who abides in Me, and I in him,*
> *bears much fruit; for without Me you can do nothing."*
> JOHN 15:5 NKJV

"Do you see where we're going with this?" God asks. "Can you trust me with your world and wait now with a purpose?"

"Oh, yes," I tell Him. "I've got it now. You do Your job and I'll do mine—with Your help. Please don't make me wait for that, too."

"Not to worry, I'm always here," He says. "I've been waiting for *you*."

# Patience is highly over-rated

My Bible doesn't say, "Those who wait on the Lord are patient," or "Those who wait on the Lord don't do anything else." It says, "Those who wait on the LORD Shall renew their strength" (Isaiah 40:31 NKJV). Shall isn't an option. Waiting and hoping in the Lord can do nothing else *but* renew my strength. Fighting Him only weakens me more.

Even in my shattered, impatient state, God can teach me and use me. Working while I wait means believing in God's ability to handle all things in His time and using the time He's given me for a purpose. I can yearn for patience, or I can wait with a purpose. It's an easy choice.

Understanding what God wants for me and how to get there is a long haul. He knows how hard it is for me sometimes. He has given me the perfect opportunities—repeatedly—and He is nothing if not diligent. Sometimes we go over the same issues again and again, as I search to rediscover His guidance or tap into His courage. My life gets in the way and I get angry and frustrated. I forget my lessons. But God doesn't forget His plan. He won't give up on me, no matter how long it takes me to learn to wait and to work on His timetable—and to stop trying to get Him to conform to mine.

God is the original multi-tasker. He tends to you and me at the same time. He is rarely accused of wasting resources, including time. Why would He have us do it? When we fret about the lack of answers and actions that we need, we waste the chance to grow. "Be still, and know that I am God," He says (Psalm 46:10 NIV). That's not patience. "Knowing" God means learning about God, drawing nearer to God, developing an unmovable trust and faith in God. That's *purpose*. That's God at work while you wait.

# Wait, but purposefully

Remember, there is a purpose, however obscured, every time you find yourself in your waiting room. You are waiting because you need to rediscover something the Lord has already given you—don't ever doubt that. When you decide to accept God's lessons, you can replace that uncomfortable impatience with life-changing purpose. Make that choice, and God will not abandon you.

> The LORD makes firm the steps
> of the one who delights in him;
> though he may stumble, he will not fall,
> for the LORD upholds him with his hand.
> PSALM 37:23–24 NIV

God wants you to come closer, but you can't do that if you're fighting Him and arguing with Him, if you can't give up the control you think you need. God's timing and your need has settled you in your waiting room for now, so accept His help. Learn what He has to teach you this time, so that you can complete your work here and then move on to another, more glorious lesson. There is no reason to be patient for your growth. God needs you to get started on your journey toward Him today.

Patience is highly over-rated, but purpose isn't. Find the purpose God has for you right now. He's waiting.

## ❖ *While You Wait* ❖

- What will you do to wait purposefully today?
- How will you work to "know God" through this wait?

........................................................................................

........................................................................................

........................................................................................

........................................................................................

........................................................................................

........................................................................................

........................................................................................

........................................................................................

........................................................................................

........................................................................................

........................................................................................

........................................................................................

........................................................................................

*Lord, please hear this prayer. You know how hard I've tried so far. You know how I've gotten in my own way. You know how I've tried to control my plans and Yours. Please help me to stop fighting and to start finding— help me to find the guidance and courage and peace I need. Help me to find purpose for every single day here with You. Help me to find understanding and appreciation of Your timing. Help me to find You.*

*We cannot comprehend God's infinite grace and how He never tires of reaching for us—we can only delight Him when we reach for Him, too.*

## PART 2

## Gathering Your Tools

*The LORD will fulfill his purpose for me;*
*your love, O LORD, endures forever—*
*do not abandon the works of your hands.*
PSALM 138:8 NKJV

CHAPTER 9—*Understanding the Wait*

Have you ever known the Lord to be unprepared? I can't imagine that He would have said, "Oh, that's right! You need food. I'm sorry, Adam, that I failed to provide it for you, and now you've nearly starved to death." How absurd. No, I don't think so.

Yet we often behave as if He's not prepared for *us*. God sees far ahead and knows what we need before we do. And just as He would not put us here without a plan, He would not give us a part in that plan without the necessary tools. I guarantee it. But first, I doubted it.

Back to God for some answers. He is infinitely patient. . . .

"Okay, Lord, I'm ready to work. I'm ready to learn how to wait purposefully. But I am ill-equipped and have no strength. What am I supposed to do this work with?"

"I'm going to tell you what you need and how to get it," He said, as calm as ever. "You will need only these three things. Trust me."

The assurance with which He spoke gave me hope, comfort, and confidence. Weren't all things possible with Him? Couldn't I learn the art of waiting purposefully if I chose to? That was what He promised, right? Getting there for me was definitely going to require some powerful tools. But the Lord said that it was possible, even guaranteed, if I would do my part as well as He was going to do His.

## What you're really waiting for

It's such a contradiction—we plead for patience when what we really want is the granting of our wishes so we don't have to be patient anymore. It's so backward. Regardless of what appears to be your goal on the outside, there is always that holier goal on the inside. The tools God's given you won't make your boss give you the promotion or the right mate appear on your doorstep—those are *external* changes—your Lord seeks the *internal* growth that moves you closer to Him, because that's the only way you can see anything clearly. I've been there, too, when I thought I was waiting for changes in others but was really waiting for changes in myself. I've complained endlessly about my lack of control over others and the lack of progress I made with my own pain. I failed to recognize the tools that God had provided to comfort me in my waiting room. That's especially easy to do when you hurt.

The wait to get through and past a difficult time in your life is perhaps the hardest kind of wait. Feeling alone and forsaken in a flood of pain, you may not be able to imagine, let alone see, the rainbow at the other end. Waiting for the pain to stop seems too much to bear. But it's a tremendous wait full of purpose and growth! The pain doesn't just stop by itself—your purposeful wait for relief from it is God's way of getting you through it. God knows that He can help you overcome the pain, if you'll let Him.

*"Come to me, all you who are weary and burdened,*
*and I will give you rest. Take my yoke upon you and learn from me,*
*for I am gentle and humble in heart,*
*and you will find rest for your souls."*
MATTHEW 11:28–29 NIV

Do you see what comes first? "Come to me. . . ," Jesus says. Do that while you wait. Reach for Him. Rest. Learn.

Don't be afraid of this painful kind of wait. We've all experienced our own tragedies of the heart that have made us ache for relief. The only way out of the pain is straight through it, with the Lord at your side. You can't go around some events in your life—disappointment in a career; failure of a marriage; the descent into unhealthy relationships or practices; hatred, bitterness, envy, or greed that has overtaken you; your own doubt and lack of faith that has hardened your heart and made you turn your back on God. These kinds of life tragedies have to be tackled head-on. You have to replace your pain with a purposeful wait as you search for the guidance, courage, and peace you've lost.

Getting through one of these kinds of waits will mean fighting the temptation to whitewash your past, but you must reveal it all. God already knows all of the gory details of any failures or mistakes you've made. He just needs you to use them now for something better—growth toward Him. Without that, you'll wait forever.

It may come as a shock for you to discover what you're really waiting for, through this wait and all the others to come. And it is always the same, through every wait, every hurt, every time you feel lost, frustrated, misguided, or afraid: you're always waiting for a closer relationship with your Lord. I know this now, and while each wait has brought me closer to God, please understand that I am forever a "work-in-progress." Don't think that I have reached some elevated status or passed a final test. I've simply learned to find a purpose amid the pain.

*So we fix our eyes not on what is seen,*
*but on what is unseen,*
*since what is seen is temporary,*
*but what is unseen is eternal.*

2 CORINTHIANS 4:18 NIV

## Building the greatest relationship

Every time you go through a wait, if you wait purposefully, you will discover the incompleteness in your relationship with God. That's the whole point—to teach you, to love you through your mistakes, to improve your vision and your compassion—to reach a more complete union. I denied to myself that my relationship with God was weak, but it was. It suffered because it was based on my giving to God only those things that I thought I could trust Him with and keeping the rest for myself, and then even taking back the few things that I did give Him when I thought that I could manage them better.

"Yes, God, I know that You have spoken the world into existence and created the intricacies of life I see before me, but I'm not sure that You can handle *my* dilemma, so I'll just take care of it myself." How sad.

I could make a list that reached from me to you of how I've misinterpreted my waiting times through the years. During some particularly difficult stages of my life, I waited without *patience* or *purpose* for others to accommodate me. I waited for those around me to understand my pain and change themselves to alleviate it. I'm sure

I wore the hinges off my waiting room door as I entered again and again to learn what I was really waiting for each time. But God was always patient, never faltering.

He is always waiting to move you closer to Him. He's not offering you a way around what hurts you or frustrates you, but a way through it, in spite of it, to a better place. The way through is in your waiting room with God. It isn't punishment; it is instruction that comes with a promise: "being confident of this, that he who began a good work in you will carry it on to completion until the day of Christ Jesus" (Philippians 1:6 NIV).

And God is so prepared. Your instruction comes with some tools, too. He's guided me with all of these tools we'll talk about here, with the infinite patience that only He possesses. These tools must come first, because you can never go forward through any wait without them. And as always, everything you need, He has supplied.

## ⁕ While You Wait ⁕

- What do you *think* you're waiting for?

- What could God need you to rediscover about your relationship with Him?

- How have you focused your waiting time on others, and how will you redirect that focus to yourself, starting today?

# CHAPTER 10—*Forgiveness*

"The first tool you'll need is forgiveness. Follow me," God said.

Isn't that just like the Lord, clean slate and all? Forgiveness, like patience, can be tough to come by for us average humans. God knew that my lack of forgiveness had caused me to wait many times over. I told Him that I was ready for this tool, *desperate* for this tool.

"Learning how to forgive is part of your work, you know," He said.

"I don't understand. How do I start? When do I start?"

"Whenever you're ready."

*Lord, make me ready.*

"This tool may be the hardest to master," God said, "but it is also the most important. You can never move forward, out of your waiting room or anywhere else, without it."

Well, don't put any pressure on me there, Lord!

God explained it all to me in easy terms for my resistant and stubborn heart.

First, I would have to forgive myself for the mistakes I had made, for anything that led me to my waiting room. That was a tall order! The hardest waits we experience are often waits to get through our own guilt. But they are also the most intimate and the ones from which we can learn the most. Before we can go forward, we must understand where we've been, even if that includes a path littered with our own mistakes. To choose to grow, to find a purpose in the difficult time, means to acknowledge our mistakes. A history of mistakes isn't bad, it's just human, but God's help is superhuman and essential to overcoming those mistakes. Accept His help. It has to come first.

# It's hard to do alone

Forgiving yourself is hard when you feel unworthy of God's help. I've been there, feeling guilt and regret that were too much to handle, feeling that I had destroyed any hope of a relationship with God. With especially difficult times in your life, it can feel as though every lesson you've ever learned has disappeared, every step you've grown closer to God has vanished. *Why would God forgive me now,* I've often wondered as I cried for peace and hope. He owed me nothing.

He didn't demand anything from me, either. Instead, He listened as I poured my heart out to Him. He listened as I cried endlessly and prayed for relief from the pain. He listened to my pleas for forgiveness when I didn't feel worthy to make them. But I couldn't listen in return. I couldn't believe that a perfect Lord could forgive imperfect me, again, this time. And if God couldn't forgive me, then I certainly couldn't forgive myself. How would I ever get out of that horrible place? How could God possibly use someone as flawed as I was? How could I ever find that path that I thought God had designed for me? Those are the most painful kinds of waits.

As I dealt with my pain over the years, I found myself time and again going to God for what I knew only He could give. Even when I thought He wouldn't listen because of my failures, I went anyway. He began to help me see Him there, not with a scorecard but a job description. If He could still find some usefulness in me, then surely He would help me to see it, too. Learning to forgive myself was not about justifying or rationalizing past mistakes. It was about learning the difference between the past and the future. When I could see that forgiveness was a tool (and a gift) that I needed to go forward, His instruction became clearer. I didn't have to feel trapped and locked in my waiting room—I could begin to see my way out. Through every wait of this kind, it seems that I have to learn how to forgive all over again, and it's not been easy.

Through the waiting, I've had to admit to God and myself the ways I've failed both of us. It was the way to leave those mistakes there, in the past. *Waiting purposefully* is all about going forward and making better choices in this wait and the others to come. The past was a textbook, nothing else. It wasn't destined to repeat itself if I could learn from it and leave it there. The learning, though, is always based on forgiveness. Without forgiveness, it's like sitting in the car with all the windows painted black—the road is there, but you can't see it. The car is useless and you get nowhere. Clear away what's blocking your view, and you reveal the path and have the means to travel it.

I had to believe that the Lord would no longer remember my shortcomings, but instead, welcome me and help me, not because I had never failed, but because I had chosen to grow again. I needed His forgiveness and mercy, and I had to trust Him to give them to me.

> *For this is what the high and exalted One says—*
> *he who lives forever, whose name is holy:*
> *"I live in a high and holy place,*
> *but also with the one who is contrite and lowly in spirit,*
> *to revive the spirit of the lowly*
> *and to revive the heart of the contrite. . . .*
> *I have seen their ways, but I will heal them;*
> *I will guide them and restore comfort."*
> ISAIAH 57:15, 18 NIV

Forgiving myself and accepting forgiveness from God had to be joined, because there could be nothing standing between us for my wait to be purposeful. As long as I resisted what God offered, I was stuck. You will be, too.

"There's one more part of this tool, you know," the Lord said.

"What more do I have to do?"

He said that I had to forgive others the grudges that I held against them. That's easy for Him, He's God.

"I'm the one who's been wronged, You know," I said, in case He missed that.

"Let it go," He ordered.

The reasoning was actually fairly simple. God said that I also had to let go of that unhealthy part of my past, the part filled with pain caused by others. I was wrong to think that their hurts against me were mine to deal with. God said that I just needed to forgive them, to "let it go," so that I could return to my work. Forgiving them in the human way I could was *my* job—everything else was *His* job. I had to stop trying to do His job. All I had to do was forgive the pain so that I could get past it. I didn't have to absolve anyone or justify anyone or even understand anyone—I just needed to get the pain out of my heart and give it to God. He's a much better judge of what to do with it than I am. I have enough to do. God can have those hurts! As He showed me how He designed it to be used, I discovered that I liked this part of the tool, after all.

*"And when you stand praying,*
*if you hold anything against anyone, forgive them,*
*so that your Father in heaven may forgive you your sins."*
MARK 11:25 NIV

Waiting purposefully is not about reforming others, but about growing *me*, working with everything that I am and knowing that God is willing to take a shot at it, too. I had to remember that God deals with us all—I only have to deal with my imperfections. I can forgive and let God have the pain and anger and disappointment. There is other work to do, other more spiritual demands to satisfy. My purposeful waiting would take all of the energy I had. There was none to spare for judging others.

"You see? You should learn from the past, not wallow in it. I know where you've been. I'm far more concerned with where you're going," God said.

How could I argue with that? How could I say no if God Himself was not yet done with me?

"Lead the way," I said.

"That's the second tool," He said.

## ⟶ While You Wait ⟵

- How do you need to use the tool of forgiveness in your waiting now?

- How do you need to forgive yourself, seek and accept God's forgiveness, or grant forgiveness to others?

- How will using the tool of forgiveness help you to wait purposefully?

# Chapter 11—*Expectation*

*Now this is the confidence that we have in Him,*
*that if we ask anything according to His will, He hears us.*
1 JOHN 5:14 NKJV

When I took a look at what the Lord had for me to do, it was frightening! The hurts in my heart felt impossible to overcome. I felt weak and inadequate. All of the effort in the world didn't seem like enough to even begin dealing with the distance I had put between God and me. But God said no.

"I know you're scared," He said. "But we have much work to do, and you will discover many wonders on the other side. You can grow through this wait. Do you believe you can?"

"It's a toss-up," I confessed.

"No, it isn't," He said. "Believe, and it will be."

The tool of expectation had two sides, too. The expectation would form the proper framework for my efforts, for my lessons. It started with God and ended with me. It works the same for you.

First, *expect* that God will be there to help you. You will not be forsaken or abandoned. What good would that do? God starts no work that He doesn't plan to finish. He isn't going away or going to change His mind after He has gotten you this far. Your wait is using *His* time, too, and He will keep you in your waiting room as long as He needs to. When you wait, you wait until you see what He wants you to see, however long that takes.

# Sometimes, it's hard to believe

In the most painful waits of my life, those that resulted from my poor judgment, I've always been afraid that God wouldn't help me because of the ways I had failed Him. It's a fairly common misconception among us impatient types that God will respond the same way other humans often do, in retaliation, holding grudges, conditionally. It isn't true.

> *Let us then approach God's throne of grace*
> *with confidence, so that we may receive mercy*
> *and find grace to help us in our time of need.*
> HEBREWS 4:16 NIV

Before I joined with God in uncovering the lessons He had to teach, I was afraid and insecure. Still, I prayed anyway. I prayed for His helping hand and doubted that He would offer it. I ached for His guidance and strength because I refused to believe that He would give it to me. I lost faith in myself and in God, too. But God doesn't work that way.

He never left my side, not for one moment, during any of my painful waits. He never planned to, but I was too afraid to believe it. I often wondered why He would bother with me where there were plenty of people far more saintly than I, eagerly awaiting His instruction. *Maybe He's just forgotten about me and isn't bothered by my intense pain. Maybe He doesn't care if I'm lost. Maybe He's dumped me for good.* Those thoughts seem logical enough at the time. I thought I was listening for Him, but I never heard Him. I confirmed my fears. I was wrong.

When you can't hear God's grace, it's because your heart has closed itself and will not listen. He is always healing you, always working on you. And when you believe again—even just the tiniest beginning—that He will always love you and help you, you will see that His grace was there all along. While you wait, believe and expect Him to follow through on everything He's told you. He is the constant you can always count on. He didn't leave me during the times that I doubted everything I'd ever known. He was just waiting for me to look ahead instead of back, waiting for me to expect what He had already guaranteed.

> So the Lord said, "If you have faith as a mustard seed,
> you can say to this mulberry tree,
> 'Be pulled up by the roots and be planted in the sea,'
> and it would obey you."
> LUKE 17:6 NKJV

## Great expectations

Expect God to be there in your wait, and then use the second part of the tool: expect to succeed in your journey. God never started anything to fail, and you won't fail at the purpose He's given you now unless you stop. Instead, keep company with the Lord and expect this waiting time to reveal a purpose far greater than you have imagined. Expect to find the reason for your stay in your waiting room, learn from it and grow nearer to God. If you're experiencing a deeply sad or frightening wait, your expectations will sustain and lead you in the right direction. Don't be afraid to expect too much from your Lord. He will use whatever you give Him.

I'm not sure what I was expecting during my waiting room years when my life had taken some unexpected turns. I think from time to time that I almost hoped God would say, "Well, okay, if this is where you are, don't bother me anymore." Then I could have more easily justified my fears and doubts and regained the control I thought I had, useless as it was. What He said instead was, "Okay, if this is where you are, you will grow and learn and see many things I could not have taught you otherwise. Pay attention. We can get where we're going from anywhere you start." He was right. Each journey has been a wild ride, but they're all the same—toward a closer relationship with Him. Give Him everything and it will come back blessed.

> *He who sows sparingly will also reap sparingly,*
> *and he who sows bountifully will also reap bountifully.*
> 2 CORINTHIANS 9:6 NKJV

Expect God's guidance while you wait and work. Expect progress and growth and happiness and success. God will not let you down in your wait, no matter how far you've fallen or how far you've strayed. With a framework of proper expectation, you are ready to listen and learn.

"Pull up your boot straps," He said. "You'll need one more thing."

## ⸙ While You Wait ⸙

- How do you need to use the tool of expectation in your waiting now?

- Where do you need to make adjustments in your expectations?

- How will using the tool of expectation help you to wait purposefully?

# Chapter 12—Commitment

~~~~~

"Now, I never said that this would be easy," God said.

Of course not, what a surprise.

Just because it's what the Lord wants me to do doesn't mean that it's the path of least resistance, mostly because the biggest obstacle in the way is *me*. How can it be easy when I have to work with myself? Forgiving myself meant dealing with my own frailties and insecurities and fears. Expecting great things of myself was terrifying. And now there was more. . . .

"This is not a standardized test, you know," God said. "There is no time limit or cheat sheet. You must commit to the work we have to do."

"Yeah, yeah, I know. Can't give up and all that. . . ," I whined.

"That's the spirit!"

He was right, of course. To clear the ground for success, expect it, and then to give up on it would be tragic. I had to hang in there to build the substance and structure of my self-work, and the commitment was the tool to help me do that.

*Commit your works to the Lord,*
*And your thoughts will be established.*
PROVERBS 16:3 NKJV

## Giving up would be easier

~~~~~

When you wait, your work is focused on the internal changes that

God needs. Those are the real reasons for your wait, and those discoveries don't come quickly. I had to be committed to allowing the discoveries in myself to come slowly, as I worked through the many stages of my wait. I had to be patient—wait, it's a catch-22! God slipped that one in on me!

Not really, He didn't. The patience was for me to have with myself as I stumbled and fell, backslid, and bobbled my way along. I couldn't give up hope during those times of setbacks (and believe me, mine could have sidelined a Roman tax collector). I had to hold on to my commitment and not give up, even when giving up seemed like the only alternative. I had to trust that God wouldn't give up on me either. I had to trust that He would be patient with my meager progress, and then help me to be patient with it as well.

Commitment meant focusing all of my control and effort on the work before me—the work *within* me. It meant slowing down long enough to listen to God and having the faith to follow through on what He told me, even when so much of my world felt as if it were spiraling out of control.

Your life may feel out of control in any number of ways, with struggles that only you can understand. Finding yourself in your waiting room can be awfully confusing sometimes, especially when it feels as if you've done the right things or made the right decisions, and yet, you find yourself waiting. Don't be afraid—it just means that you're waiting for *something else* before you can move forward. Commit yourself to finding that purpose and moving nearer to the Lord. Then all of the noise around you will do one of two things: it will begin to make sense or it won't matter. When your focus and commitment is on God's work, then you can wait purposefully. Jesus said it simply: "You follow Me" (John 21:22 NKJV). Make a commitment to take even one step. Step in His direction, and understand your wait.

Understanding isn't always easy. Through different trials of my life, I've fought draining feelings of anger and resentment, fear and confusion. I've cursed the world I built because I couldn't make it what I wanted it to be, *instantly!* Sometimes, I would think that God had finally decided to leave me in my pain, forsaken. I would attack the unhappiness around me like a swarm of yellow jackets that could be swatted down with enough force and a good arm. I was waiting (not very patiently or purposefully) for God and everyone else to conform to my expectations. I was working so hard to build and escape at the same time. My days were just too demanding—God should have known that, I decided, with fear and mistrust. God *did* know that, but He also knew that the purposeful wait I needed was about changing *me*, moving *me*, not what I thought it was. I wanted to stop trying so hard to get past the pain because it all hurt so much. God said, "Don't give up, just go through the pain."

"Make the commitment, and I won't leave you to do your work alone," He said.

"But I hurt, I'm afraid, I need help," I cried.

"I know."

> *"The one who comes to Me*
> *I will by no means cast out."*
> JOHN 6:37 NKJV

When I chose to look *in* instead of *out* for my peace and rest, God was there, waiting. He showed me how to be more understanding, less judgmental, how to focus on the path He and I traveled together. If you don't believe that God can use you wherever you are, then you are blinded to His help. I began to focus on what I could change about *me* to make my life better, to bring me closer to God and closer to seeing His plan for me.

A resolved commitment didn't mean that I would awake one day with no more complications in my very stressful life. It meant that I was determined to find ways to grow within the complications and to use those times of waiting to move closer to my Lord. The purpose for my wait might seem hidden or elusive, but I was committed to finding it.

## ❖ While You Wait ❖

- How do you need to use the tool of commitment in your waiting now?

- What are you afraid of committing to, and how has it held you back, away from God?

- How will using the tool of commitment help you to wait purposefully?

# CHAPTER 13—*The Tools Are Forever Renewable*

No matter what you need to happen in your life, or what trauma you need to get through, or what inside work you're so desperately waiting for, God is prepared for you. These tools of forgiveness, expectation, and commitment are never breakable or hidden. God provides them for us because He knows our weakness. He knows our very human need for order and logic, for guidelines and supplies. He's had the tools there for us all along, yet sometimes we are unbelievably slow to recognize them. Why is that, because it seems too easy to think that the Lord would supply us with what we need, at the mere breath of a request?

No, I think we fail to see these gifts because we are looking in the wrong place. We are looking at ourselves to supply the first part of our growth, when the first part always comes from God—forgiveness for us, a promise of help, and the patience to work and wait with us. All we have to do is ask. These gifts are everlasting and cannot be depleted. The manna falls every day. When you look to God first, then you see what you need to supply as well. It always starts with one step toward Him.

*My soul, wait silently for God alone,*
*For my expectation is from Him,*
*He only is my rock and my salvation;*
*He is my defense;*
*I shall not be moved.*
*In God is my salvation and my glory;*
*The rock of my strength,*
*And my refuge, is in God.*
PSALM 62:5–7 NKJV

## Impatient, again. . .

With an understanding of my tools, I was anxious to get to work. I wanted and needed results *now*, immediate evidence of my efforts. That bit of impatience was no big surprise for God or me. But He said that I still wasn't ready, not just yet. The next step was the beginning of it all, the foundation of my purpose. I had to listen more, to Him and to myself. He said that I had to learn who I am.

"Now, let's begin," He said.

### ꙮ While You Wait ꙮ

-   How will you trust that God is prepared for your wait?

-   How will you let Him know that you've accepted *His* part in your wait first?

-   Talk to God about using your tools as you begin *your* part of the wait.

........................................................................................

........................................................................................

........................................................................................

........................................................................................

........................................................................................

........................................................................................

......................................................................................................................

......................................................................................................................

......................................................................................................................

......................................................................................................................

......................................................................................................................

......................................................................................................................

......................................................................................................................

......................................................................................................................

......................................................................................................................

......................................................................................................................

......................................................................................................................

......................................................................................................................

......................................................................................................................

......................................................................................................................

*Lord, this is frightening. It means questioning everything I think I know. It means admitting those failures and mistakes I'd rather forget. It means destroying what I've been standing on to lean unto You. It means trying, again and again, to follow You, desperately listening for Your words. Please help me hear You. Please help me trust what I hear. Please help me.*

*God will meet you much closer than halfway, but you must keep going in the right direction—toward Him.*

## PART 3

# Knowing Who You Are

*"Ask and it will be given to you; seek and you will find;*
*knock and the door will be opened to you.*
*For everyone who asks receives; the one who seeks finds;*
*and to the one who knocks, the door will be opened."*
MATTHEW 7:7–8 NIV

## CHAPTER 14—Learning to Listen

"In every wait, part of the purpose is learning who you are," God said, as if I were supposed to understand that.

"Well, I've lived with me forever. Don't You think I already know that?" I asked, hoping to skip this step.

"Apparently not. But this wait and all the others will get you closer to knowing and understanding—if you will slow down long enough to learn."

"Slow down? I'm *stopped*, remember?" He had clearly lost track of my problem. . . .

"You're never stopped. You're always moving. All that matters is the direction."

"Even when I have to wait?"

"*Especially* when you have to wait."

"Well, that's clear as fog in a hollow. Could You help me out a little bit, Lord?"

"That's what I'm here for."

Again, God told me that He was going to help me, that I wouldn't have to learn all of this alone. He told me that a great part of waiting purposefully is wrapped up in learning who I am so that I will know who I can become, the answers revealing themselves through each agonizing wait. I was quite sure that He had nodded off a little in that proclamation, but I was wrong. Again. Imagine that.

When you're going through a difficult time, waiting for acceptance or affirmation, strength or understanding, it's easy to lose perspective. You can feel like you don't know anything anymore. Everything must begin anew. Everything must be learned as God intended, not as you had orchestrated on your own.

A painful wait will often reveal a truckload of new information about your relationship with God. Before one of my most difficult waits, I thought I knew how to listen to Him pretty well. With the exception of a few moments of true clarity and connection, though, I wasn't really listening because I didn't think it was necessary all the time. Prayer was official and in desperation. Worship was formal and organized. My view was distorted and my hearing was weak. I had not listened with expectation.

As you work through your wait, make listening as God talks to you not a separate activity you do each day, but a part of you that is as automatic as your breathing. It is life-giving. It is part of the relationship you crave, and the Lord will not withhold His words.

*For I know the thoughts that I think toward you, says the LORD,*
*thoughts of peace and not of evil, to give you a future and a hope.*
*Then you will call upon Me and go and pray to Me,*
*and I will listen to you.*
JEREMIAH 29:11–13 NKJV

# Slow down

Every time I'm ill and impatient, it becomes clear that I've pushed God away. Our conversations have become strained, consisting mainly of me demanding yet another blessing or taking one second to breathe a prayer of thanks. There is no dialog, no growth, no real interaction because I resist it. In my little fits of power (we delude ourselves so easily sometimes), I would let God stay on His side of the world and I would stay on mine, unless I needed Him in a pinch, of course. What an ungrateful child I could be!

Then another painful wait would find me, and I would run to Him, crying, seeking answers and questioning His judgment. He was always there, but for so long, I could not or *would* not see the blessings of my waiting room. "Slow down," He finally said loud enough for me to hear. "You're going to learn something while you wait." Yes, Sir.

Slowing down is the beginning of a purposeful wait. It seems as if you're losing even more ground, but you're not. You will find great peace and comfort in focusing solely on listening to God—not for the answers you've already ordered, but for the lessons He has to teach.

Be willing to listen carefully, with an open and calm heart, because He will not shout very often. Make listening a blessed habit, listening because you expect Him to tell you something you need to know. Forming or reestablishing this habit is always part of your waiting times. It is a habit that you can practice and that gets easier and far more effective over time.

Start practicing the habit of listening to God as soon as you wake in the morning. Greet each day with a pause to listen to God. Don't tear out in a rush to fight your wait. Slow down and listen. Quietly, by yourself, just sit and listen for a few moments. Think about drawing nearer to God and feel Him wrap His arms around you and welcome you to your day. Anticipate and expect growing closer to your Lord.

What you'll find when you do this is that God has been talking to you all along. You've just failed to listen, and it's been your loss. Fortunately, it's a loss that you can rectify instantly. You can continue your life without benefit of hearing Him, or you can take a moment to listen and learn, your choice. You can bet that He's listening to *you*.

> *Let the morning bring me word of your unfailing love,*
> *for I have put my trust in you.*
> *Show me the way I should go,*
> *for to you I entrust my life.*
> PSALM 143:8 NIV

## ⸎ While You Wait ⸎

- Can you remember a wonderful time when God spoke to you?

- How can you apply what you learned then to what you need to learn now?

# CHAPTER 15—Talk to Him

Sometimes, we consider prayer a formal entreaty to the Lord for favors or blessings, a time of praise and confession. That's true, but it's incomplete. Any time that we talk to God is prayer, because He is all that there is, so whatever we do is wrapped up in Him. Still, there is more than one way to pray, or rather, there is more that can be considered prayer than what you may have thought. God is never so one-dimensional.

Try an experiment, or begin this practice again if you've let this part of your life fade away. When a new thought goes through your mind today and you need to consider several choices or make a quick decision, talk to God about it. I guarantee that He's interested, and you can practice listening.

Your experiment doesn't have to include life-altering decisions, or even particularly important thoughts. The idea is to stop and talk to God about what is happening in your life. Wherever you are, stop and tell Him what you're thinking—to clarify it for *you* (He already knows). Then listen. Feel His response. Go on your way.

Do this regularly for a few days, and soon, this practice will become a part of you—a welcomed habit that brings you tremendous comfort and blessings. It will become part of your active prayer, and you don't have to wait. Just recognize the power of talking to God, and you'll be amazed at His response time.

*But as for me, I am poor and needy;*
*come quickly to me, O God.*
*You are my help and my deliverer;*
*Lord, do not delay.*
PSALM 70:5 NIV

# Write it down

Talking and listening to the Lord throughout the day is a wonderful part of your purposeful wait. Do it all day long, with every heartbeat, and at least once a day, every day, have a cup of coffee with God—or maybe it's tea or carrot juice, whatever you like. Perhaps you already have a devotional time. Perhaps you already write in a journal. These are wonderful ways to be close to God, and this is yet another. It is a dialog, not a report or petition.

Think of the "coffee time" as a debate team match. I know that may sound blasphemous in a way, but I don't think that God wants a passive subject. I think He wants an active participant. Why else would He make Himself available to us in our most clumsy attempts at self-discovery if He didn't want us to actively reach for Him, and to reach without fear? Don't doubt that He will welcome you. He's there, waiting.

Save your timid disposition for another time and place. Waiting purposefully means going forth in boldness, seeking God through the doubts. There is no question God will duck, no battle He can't win, no topic He doesn't know. You can't make Him uncomfortable. You can't push Him too hard. So go ahead, hit Him with your best shot. He will still be there, unmoved and unshaken, lighting your way. Then if you'll slow down and listen, you will find what you need.

*You, Lord, keep my lamp burning;*
*my God turns my darkness into light.*
*With your help I can advance against a troop;*
*with my God I can scale a wall.*
PSALM 18:28–29 NIV

# A coffeebook for you and God

I call the place where I write these times with God my *coffeebook*, because *journal* seems too broad and *notebook* seems too academic. Your coffeebook will hold yet another focus for you. It will become both history and road map for your life.

Sometimes, the only way we stubborn souls can learn is by debate. We all have a little Thomas in us. In the safety of your coffeebook, you can argue your points and search for answers. Worship doesn't mean silent acceptance. It means going to God the loving Father in comfort and knowing that He will not ignore you.

Just as importantly, as you write to God about how you feel about your wait, you will begin to know who you are and learn more of what He has planned for you. Even if you think you already know, you will be amazed at what God has to show you. It's the difference between holding a glass of water and standing in the ocean.

*For the word of God is alive and active.*
*Sharper than any double-edged sword,*
*it penetrates even to dividing soul and spirit,*
*joints and marrow; it judges the thoughts*
*and attitudes of the heart. Nothing in all creation*
*is hidden from God's sight. Everything is uncovered*
*and laid bare before the eyes of him*
*to whom we must give account.*
HEBREWS 4:12–13 NIV

## ❧ *While You Wait* ❧

— What have you been afraid to talk to God about in the past?

— Write about your experiments with listening for God in the small decisions you make this week.

— What do you want from your coffeebook time with God?

# Chapter 16—*The Coffeebook Rules*

*You have searched me, LORD,*
*and you know me.*
*You know when I sit and when I rise;*
*you perceive my thoughts from afar.*
*You discern my going out and my lying down;*
*you are familiar with all my ways.*
*Before a word is on my tongue*
*you, LORD, know it completely.*
PSALM 139:1–4 NIV

Your waiting room is just for you, and mine is for me. Your lessons are yours and mine are mine. Your path to God is interrupted by the debris you've put there, and I have sabotaged my own. So while each of us has a separate wait, there are a few rules that apply to the coffeebook time for all of us.

*Be honest.* Your coffeebook is not a place for best impressions—God already knows what you're going to write anyway. This writing is for *you.* Listen to yourself and write down what you hear. Don't be afraid. Don't judge your heart.

*The LORD is near to all who call upon Him,*
*To all who call upon Him in truth.*
PSALM 145:18 NKJV

As you begin your coffeebook, go back to the question of why you're in your waiting room. Look at both reasons—the outward change that you want in your life, of course, but more importantly, the internal discoveries that God needs you to make. Ask yourself how you honestly feel about your life right now and why you feel that way. You don't have to dictate a novel in one sitting, but you can listen a little each day and learn more about who you are.

You may wonder why that's so important, but it becomes very clear. As you learn more about you who you are, you make better choices about where you should be. God will help you see your part in His plan, the part that only *you* can play. You can't do that when you're not being your true self, and you can't learn who your true self is unless you listen to God, the One who made you, "For we are God's handiwork, created in Christ Jesus to do good works, which God prepared in advance for us to do" (Ephesians 2:10 NIV).

Perhaps you've thought, incorrectly, as it turned out, that you wanted to behave a certain way or accomplish a certain feat, and then you failed. You were devastated, but you shouldn't have been. We fail repeatedly when we don't know who we are and when we try to be someone else, when we aren't honest with ourselves. I've certainly been there. I've failed at jobs and other business ventures so many times, all the while praying and waiting for success that would never come.

Those failures cut through to my heart and frustrated and discouraged me. After I had a chance to recover and evaluate each failure, though, I saw that it wasn't the greatest choice I could have made to begin with. It wasn't *me*, and yet, I thought it would work because it seemed like a good idea at the time. In fact, it was never who I was, and that's why it failed, but the time wasn't wasted because I learned so much. If you've experienced similar failures, you know what I'm talking about. It is a tremendous feeling of loss and inadequacy. But God says no. He says it's *instruction*.

He has given us plenty to work with, but we must work within the confines of *who we are*. You can't accomplish my work, and I can't do yours. That's okay. That's the plan because "There are different kinds of working, but in all of them and in everyone it is the same God at work" (1 Corinthians 12:6 NIV). The work God has for you is stacked up, waiting for you. If you want to know what that is—the work that's especially for *you*—then listen. You can't do your work until you know who you are, the *you* that God already sees and that you will discover, the *you* that has a job waiting to be done.

## Plead your case.

Sometimes, just as with learning who you are, it's hard to specify and categorize what you want when you have no focus to your requests. I can go back and read my writing in my coffeebook and count the word "please" about a thousand times a month. "Please this and please that," I go on page after page. It isn't greed—it's conviction. Writing down those pleadings forces me to decide what I really want, what is truly in my heart. Asking for what I want is part of learning who I am, and it changes as I grow closer to God. It works the same for you, too. Here's how.

> *I cry out to the LORD with my voice;*
> *With my voice to the LORD I make my supplication.*
> *I pour out my complaint before Him;*
> *I declare before Him my trouble.*
> PSALM 142:1–2 NKJV

The act of writing down your every plea clarifies and magnifies your thoughts. Sometimes, we say we want something, but maybe we don't. Sometimes, we want something so badly that we're afraid to say it at all. Sometimes, I've found that the more I plead for something, the more or less important it becomes, depending on God's plan for me. That's when I'm learning and God is teaching, when His timing feels especially sacred. Through this unrelenting search for ourselves, we are blessed to discover what God wants to give us.

So work to discover what you want. Is it what God has in mind for you? I don't know, and you won't either until you discuss it with Him. Go to Him and discover His plans for you. He will let you know. You will learn much more than you ever imagined.

*But if from there you seek the LORD your God,*
*you will find him if you seek him with all your heart*
*and with all your soul. When you are in distress*
*and all these things have happened to you,*
*then in later days you will return*
*to the Lord your God and obey him.*
DEUTERONOMY 4:29–30 NIV

Once you've opened your heart in honesty about yourself and your desires, you'll then be able to hear what God has to say. He can't talk to you about something that you haven't claimed as your own, so use your coffeebook as a divining rod and find the well of God's wisdom.

## Pay attention.

As you get to know who you are, you will recognize when God sends you answers. You'll see that many times, you neglected to use what you learned in the past, even though it was plainly there. The lessons are hard to follow when they are new and painful, but they illuminate like a thousand lanterns the ones to come if you will only let their clarity shine on your path. Today does not stop and start. It is the continuation of yesterday and the preliminary to tomorrow. It all continues for a reason.

The past will prepare you for the future if you will listen to those lessons. One of the reasons we spend so much time stalled and waiting is that we failed to learn what God tried to teach us in the last similar circumstance. So He sits us in the waiting room again and again until we finally get it. The signs are there, but we refuse to read.

If you continue to find yourself frustrated in a certain type of relationship or job or other situation, perhaps it's because it's not *who you are*, who God means for you to be. You continue to put yourself in the wrong places and then refuse to see the unwelcome results as a call for change. Then you wait through the pain and loss and confusion while God is waiting for you to find a purpose for it all. Your frustration mounts, and you can't overcome it because you won't stop long enough to pay attention to and trust what God is trying to tell you, even though He lets you ask all the questions you want and will never lie to you.

*Test all things; hold fast what is good.*
1 THESSALONIANS 5:21 NKJV

The past isn't there just to fill up history books. It is an endless spring of self-knowledge if you will drink from it. Before you go forward, you must look back and see what worked and what didn't, what made you happy and what didn't, what brought you closer to God and what didn't. Pay attention to your history, improve your present, unlimit your future. God has the time.

# Write your praises.

Remember that you are not in this wait alone, even though it may feel that way at times because it hurts so much. Waiting purposefully is a very solitary, unique work, but you always have your permanent partner in God. Hang on to that.

Fortunately, in my coffeebook next to all of the pleadings and questions and complaints, I can find many lines of gratitude as well. Opportunities abound daily to give thanks to the Lord. Little things or big things, it doesn't matter. God delights in our happiness and is supremely pleased when we find joy in unexpected places, when we take the time to recognize the blessings He has breathed our way. These recognitions are a glorious part of your waiting room.

The thank-yous will help you to see the Lord's never-ending patience with you as you struggle with such a difficult task. Reminding yourself of the goodness and generosity of God, especially during the times you stumble and struggle, will sustain you. You will begin to recognize that He has not let you down in the past and He won't let you down in the future, despite your shortcomings and mistakes, despite what you interpret as failures. God calls it all *work*.

In your coffeebook and in your heart, praise God for the many blessings you receive each day, for every answered prayer and every wonderful gift that He gives. Thank Him for not giving up on you.

*Great is the LORD and most worthy of praise;*
*his greatness no one can fathom.*
*One generation commends your works to another;*
*they tell of your mighty acts.*
*They speak of the glorious splendor of your majesty—*

## Formatting is easy

Of course, your coffeebook doesn't have to follow any formatting rules. A spiral notebook is fine. You can write in the margins, use incomplete sentences, even misspell—doesn't matter to God. But you may find yourself following a couple of patterns. I'll tell you about a couple of mine.

When I start a new coffeebook, I always put the entire date on the cover and the first page. When that coffeebook is full, I put the year on the last entry, too, for easy reference.

I always date the top of the other pages with the day of the week and the date: Friday, September 6. Each page usually begins, "Hello, Lord, please hear my prayers." It just feels like the best way to start. Then each page ends with "love, Karon," in case He confuses me with some other impatient child of His!

And then at the very end, there is one line I always add. "And God said. . ." I put that there to remind myself that He is listening. I know that He will always answer me. I know that He has a plan and that in some way, He will talk to me and reveal to me what I need to hear and what I should do. He will answer you, too.

*Then you shall call, and the LORD will answer;*
*You shall cry, and He will say, "Here I am."*
ISAIAH 58:9 NKJV

## ❧ While You Wait ❧

- How will you trust God to take part in your coffeebook discussions?

- Write honestly about your confusion and anxiety in your wait, and listen for God's reply.

- Offer the Lord thanks for one blessing He has given to you today. I challenge you to stop at just one!

.........................................................................................................

.........................................................................................................

.........................................................................................................

.........................................................................................................

.........................................................................................................

.........................................................................................................

.........................................................................................................

.........................................................................................................

.........................................................................................................

.........................................................................................................

.........................................................................................................

.........................................................................................................

## CHAPTER 17—*God's Timing, My Wait*

*How long, LORD? Will you forget me forever?*
*How long will you hide your face from me?*
*But I trust in your unfailing love;*
*my heart rejoices in your salvation.*
PSALM 13:1, 5 NIV

Sometimes, I think God gives you a sneak preview of His plans, but the implausibility is so great that you file the hope away along with the chances of winning the Nobel Prize. I'll tell you about one of my hopes that began long, long ago.

Since writing with a pencil was far more common than composing on a keyboard, writing was all I ever wanted to do. Always, it was a dream, always in my heart. I didn't know where it came from, but I couldn't deny it. The pursuit took me through newspaper journalism (which I loved), marketing (which I hated), and technical work (which was okay), but none of it was ever the kind of writing I craved to do.

Somewhere, sometime farther back than I can even remember and though I never said it out loud, I allowed myself a bigger dream and hope, one that I could not tell a soul (and still did not verbalize to anyone other than my editor until this book you're holding was in the works!). I wanted to write books just like this one, books of Christian growth and inspiration. Forever logical, though, I relegated that dream to an impossible, hopeless wish that I must surely have been crazy to ever imagine.

The possibility simply made no sense. I was no Bible scholar by any means. And I had made it a good way through my life without any horrible misfortunes or disadvantages that sometimes provoke

Christian understanding. What made me think that I would ever have a message to share with anyone else? All I had was the hope that God would make this dream possible, and sometimes, I would be brave (or foolish) enough to believe that it could happen. Then suffering through the hardest parts of my life when I felt completely forsaken and lost, I decided that I had been terribly mistaken all along. The hope of writing the books I wanted to write was a cruel joke on my heart. In such desperate need of help myself, I could never offer any inspiration to anyone else. My dream had shattered into a million pieces, along with my life, and I doubted that God would want me to do the only thing I'd really ever wanted to do my entire life. But maybe I was wrong.

We all have those hard experiences sooner or later, and during some terrifying years of my life, God found me and picked me up so that I could search for Him again. It had been decades since I first had the dream of writing the books I wanted to write, and it felt like a lifetime since I had even revisited that dream. Then, slowly, in God's time, He brought me through those hardest and most painful years, and I began to let the dream resurface. This time, it had more structure, it felt more possible. This time, it came with a *purpose*. The time was finally right.

There was a foundation for my dream besides my blind longing. God's timing had saved this purpose for me until I could understand it. That's what He *does*—it's His timing that matters. The wait was long, and often I thought that God had ignored my pleas. His view of the timing, though, was far more expansive than mine. Everything from the time I bore my dream to its realization was part of my purposeful wait—and what a long wait it was! But that's okay, too, because the Lord's timing is infallible.

His timing allows for all possibilities in our lives, and He puts us in our waiting rooms so that we can see them. Wait. Look. God may be sending you your dream.

*Trust in the LORD, and do good;*
*Dwell in the land, and feed on His faithfulness.*
*Delight yourself also in the LORD,*
*And He shall give you the desires of your heart.*
*Commit your way to the LORD,*
*Trust also in Him, And He shall bring it to pass.*
*He shall bring forth your righteousness as the light,*
*And your justice as the noonday.*
PSALM 37:3–6 NKJV

## ❧ While You Wait ❧

- Can you look back through your life at how some difficult waits have actually propelled you toward a dream?

- How could this wait be part of a dream now?

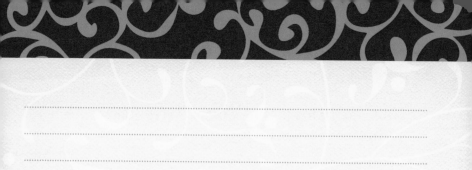

## CHAPTER 18—*Why You're Here*

I'll guess and say that you're reading this book now because you want to grow in your relationship with God, because you want help during a difficult time, because you're waiting on your dream—because waiting drives you crazy! You want to be a better disciple, but it's a constant struggle, rooted in your humanity yet supported by your spirit. Take heart, it is a struggle you can win because of God's grace and unending help.

Winning isn't easy, though, and God expects you to do more than show up for the game. He's there to listen and coach, lead and direct. But you have to talk to Him. You have to reach out to Him for counsel and companionship. You have to risk stinging failure on the way to sweet success, risk hurdling two steps forward and falling three steps back as you work to find your way. He knows it's a long journey, but He's not going anywhere and you won't be alone.

> *Those who know your name will trust in you, for you,*
> *Lord, have never forsaken those who seek you.*
> PSALM 9:10 NIV

God knows that we cannot even begin to fathom His universal plan, that we can't even correctly grasp our own part in it much of the time. He knows that we need opportunity after opportunity to reach for Him, example after example to understand. He knows that the best time to grow us is when we wait. We are terminally inclined to *do*, to *seek*, to *find*.

"No problem," God says, "*do* the work I've given you, *seek* to know me and to know yourself, *find* your way through this wait and grow nearer to me on the other side—that is always your purpose."

He's talking to you when He says that, when He challenges us to grow. You've taken the first step. Welcome to your blessed waiting room. God is in charge.

## What we all need

When you talk to God each day and write to Him in your coffeebook, don't be ashamed of the qualities you lack. Don't be bothered by where you start.

> *Who shall separate us from the love of Christ?*
> *Shall trouble or hardship or persecution or famine*
> *or nakedness or danger or sword?. . . For I am convinced*
> *that neither death nor life, neither angels nor demons,*
> *neither the present nor the future, nor any powers,*
> *neither height nor depth, nor anything else in all creation,*
> *will be able to separate us from the*
> *love of God that is in Christ Jesus our Lord.*
> ROMANS 8:35, 38–39 NIV

No matter what your specific need is right now, your wait includes rediscovering something that God has already given you, something that is hidden. Perhaps you've lost your grip on one of those things that we all misplace from time to time. Do you need guidance? Courage? Peace? They're all there in your waiting room. I promise. *Shh*—listen, trust, and believe. Draw yourself closer to the Lord every second of your wait. What a beautiful use for your time.

## ∻ While You Wait ∻

- How will you talk to God every day and try to learn who you are?

- What have you misplaced, and how will you use this wait to rediscover it?

........................................................................

........................................................................

........................................................................

........................................................................

........................................................................

........................................................................

........................................................................

........................................................................

........................................................................

........................................................................

........................................................................

........................................................................

........................................................................

........................................................................

........................................................................

........................................................................

........................................................................

........................................................................

..........................................................................................................

..........................................................................................................

..........................................................................................................

..........................................................................................................

..........................................................................................................

..........................................................................................................

..........................................................................................................

..........................................................................................................

..........................................................................................................

..........................................................................................................

..........................................................................................................

*Lord, I know that You will help me. I have blocked my way to You and to myself for so long because I've failed to listen to You. Please help me to reveal to myself the parts that I have been too blind to see, and help me to shape them into what You would have me to be. That's who I want to be. I want to be Your own one that You have called, that You haven't given up on, with all the confidence and security of a loved child. Help me to know who I am, so that I can know who I can become for You.*

*God has wonderful plans for you, the only you He made. Trust Him to prepare the way, and trust Him not to be late.*

## PART 4

## Rediscovering the Guidance
## That's Hidden by Doubt

*Trust in the LORD with all your heart,*
*And lean not on your own understanding;*
*In all your ways acknowledge Him,*
*And He shall direct your paths.*
PROVERBS 3:5–6 NKJV

## CHAPTER 19—*Lost in Doubt*

"Let me guess. You're frustrated with your wait right now, aren't you?" the Lord asks, as if He ever has to guess *anything*.

"Well, yes," I confess. "Sometimes, I feel like I'm waiting for Your answers and they won't come. I'm always waiting for things to happen or for my plans to work out, and it feels like the more I go forward, the more I fall back. I feel lost. What's wrong with me?"

"You *are* lost. You're waiting for the wrong thing," He says.

"What's the right thing?"

"To rediscover your trust in me to lead you where you need to go."

"But I've been waiting, and I can't see Your guidance. Why can't I?"

"Because you're looking at the destination. I'm talking about the journey."

"But what do I do now? How do I make the journey through this waiting time?"

"The same way you get through them all. I will guide you. You need not doubt."

I heard my Lord say those words, so why could I not trust Him and feel His instruction in my heart? God said that His guidance was there all along. I just had to overcome my doubt to find it. That seemed almost impossible when what I wanted so badly was a quick end to my wait. God had a better plan, and now was the time to join Him.

*I will instruct you and teach you in the way you should go;*
*I will guide you with My eye.*
PSALM 32:8 NKJV

I *was* making progress by the time we arrived at the wait that prompted this search. I had learned a bit about waiting purposefully, that it meant more learning and more letting go as I worked through the outward wait. There was something very important, some growth just for me that God had in mind, and I would discover it. This time, I only had to banish the doubt that had grown between Him and me, yes, *only*. The Lord certainly knows how to get your attention and, if nothing else, conversing with Him shows you real quickly who has wavered from the cause or lost sight of the path!

There was one command for this wait, and it came with a promise: "Call to Me, and I will answer you, and show you great and mighty things, which you do not know" (Jeremiah 33:3 NKJV). Wow. What a payoff. And all I had to do was ask.

## What you need, what you want

"Why have you doubted me?" God wants to know.

Sometimes, He just won't let you by without an explanation.

"I was afraid. As much as I've doubted Your willingness to guide, I've doubted my ability to hear," I told Him.

"Why must you make things so hard on yourself? Don't you know I have already worked out this and every other concern you have? It's just up to you to listen."

When He put it that way, it was hard to doubt anything.

"We have to remove your doubt, so that you can discover so much more."

*If any of you lacks wisdom, you should ask God,*
*who gives generously to all without finding fault,*
*and it will be given to you. But when you ask,*
*you must believe and not doubt, because the one who doubts*
*is like a wave of the sea, blown and tossed by the wind.*
JAMES 1:5–6 NIV

It's so odd that we would doubt something God never intended to withhold from us—His guiding touch that holds the world in motion and keeps the winds at bay. He gave us eyes and ears to appreciate and share the beauty of the world He built, not to chart our course— that's what our *hearts* are for. It is with our hearts that we listen for His guidance and trust His lead, one step at a time. It is with our hearts that we truly see and hear.

Still, it's so easy to doubt in the trenches, in the fear and the uncertainty that surrounds us when we wait, especially for something big, such as a job or relationship or the fulfillment of a dream. These outward waits make us curse the time and complain impatiently. All the while, God is saying, "Don't panic, your time is not being wasted, we have much to do, but you must listen. . . ."

We don't want to have to slow down and listen. We just want to be quickly enlightened, answered, blessed. But listening for God's guidance is a habit that we must cultivate, and it takes work. Often it takes a wait to secure our full attention to making the doubt disappear. So God says, "Yes, rediscover my guidance now by rediscovering your trust—we will use this time."

## Listening

Listening for the Lord's guidance isn't about sitting quietly and expecting trumpets and voices from above. It's about humbling yourself, clearing your mind and your heart of what you *think* you know, and trusting God to show you what you *need* to know.

But if you doubt God and rely on yourself, your can't tap into what He's given you and see where He wants you to go. He will not withhold His guidance, because it's *already there*—everything you will ever need is *already there*. But you must rediscover it to use it. You must listen and follow, like the sheep for their shepherd, without question.

"And when [the shepherd] brings out his own sheep, he goes before them; and the sheep follow him, for they know his voice" (John 10:4 NKJV). What a comfort—to have the Lord go out before me so that I can follow in complete trust, with my heart. It's no coincidence that we see Jesus as a shepherd. What more caring and compassionate figure is there than a shepherd, and what creature is more helpless and in need of guidance than a sheep? That's me. Maybe that's you, too.

God is so eager to reveal the guidance you need for the journey that He has for you. He wants you to share what He's blessed into your heart and to touch with the hand that holds His, to have a "walk worthy of the Lord, fully pleasing Him, being fruitful in every good work and increasing in the knowledge of God" (Colossians 1:10 NKJV).

So while you wait on the events that you want in your life, replace your doubt with a faith that pleases the Lord, one heartbeat at a time. The tangible things of your life will come or not, but the growth in your relationship with your Lord will not be ignored. Wait purposefully by letting God guide you where you need to go.

I can't tell you what plans the Lord has for you, or that you will always understand them immediately, but I can tell you that you can know what to do each day—*this day's work*. That's enough. That's all you need. When you ask God for His guidance on a big wait, He will uncover it for you, without fail. But He will show it to you in ways that you can understand and in increments that you can handle—one day's worth of God's wisdom is about all any of us can absorb at a time! He knows that. He just wants you to know it, too, and trust that that is enough. You never have to doubt His view of your waiting room.

> *A man's heart plans his way,*
> *But the LORD directs his steps.*
> PROVERBS 16:9 NKJV

That's the tough part, though, isn't it? How do we wait for those instructions and then believe them when they come?

## ⋟ While You Wait ⋞

- → How have you doubted God's guidance in your life and through your waits?

- → Why do you doubt now?

- → How will you listen with your heart for God's guidance today?

# CHAPTER 20—*Surrendering the Doubt*

*Search me, God, and know my heart;*
*test me and know my anxious thoughts.*
*See if there is any offensive way in me,*
*and lead me in the way everlasting.*

PSALM 139:23–24 NIV

How do you surrender and believe, accept and follow God's guidance? Is it obvious? Not always. Complicated? Not likely. Guaranteed? Of course. God has promised to help us, not just on Sundays or when we're ill or when we have life-altering decisions to make, but forever. "Lo, I am with you always," Jesus said (Matthew 28:20 NKJV). I don't read any qualifying remarks there, do you? My Bible says "always," and there is no double meaning or outdated definition for that word. So if the Lord's going to hang around and help me, why would I fight Him? Why would you? I think I know. It's so hard to trust and surrender our doubt because it goes against our human quest for control and command of all we touch. We have trouble with accepting that which we cannot see.

I've fought the Lord all my life and doubted His power time and again, but through each wait, He's helped me get closer to Him so that I don't fight as hard or doubt as much the next time. He is forever patient with my spirit, the spirit that comes with a stubborn streak we both have to deal with!

"You could make this easier, you know," He says.

"And spoil Your entertainment. . . ?" He gives me a good view of my own laughable arm-flailing every now and then.

And so we settle down in my waiting room again, patient God and impatient me.

Where do we start when we need to listen for God's guidance, with pain and confusion so heavy on our hearts? Surrendering your doubt to the Lord can seem like an impossible task when so many questions and fears are pressing on your mind. It can be easy to think that God's guidance and instruction are unavailable when you're waiting through a difficult time, and you wonder how you'll ever be able to hear Him through your doubt.

Sometimes, if we're responsible for our pain and our wait, it's especially easy to doubt, and we wonder when and how we can begin to hear and follow God's guidance that we've ignored for so long. The answer is now and with God's grace, and it always comes in a wait. Again, it feels easier to doubt Him than trust Him, but God is stronger than your doubt.

*Teach me to do your will,*
*for you are my God;*
*may your good Spirit*
*lead me on level ground.*
PSALM 143:10 NIV

God is there, still, always, *especially* when you're hurting, ready to cradle you close when you finally surrender to Him. And you do that by resting your head on His shoulder and listening with your heart. When we wait for wounds to heal or bad feelings to subside or fears to go away, we feel unsure, afraid, not knowing where to turn. Turn to God and ask for the guidance you need—*for today*. Remember that's how you start to surrender—by giving God *this day*. You wait purposefully by starting with *today*.

You can wait for better times while you rediscover the joy of a total dependence on the Lord. You can wait for answers while you listen to the one-step-at-a-time guidance that He gives if you ask.

He won't give you the directions in code or so fast that you can't write them down. No, He will reveal to you the guidance you need today so that you can get to tomorrow, and then tomorrow, He will give you the guidance to get to the next day. Each day's work is a step far more important than how it affects your external wait. It holds the growth toward God that you can only experience when you slow down and let Him lead you. Learning to follow His guidance through each day's work is always, *always* part of the real reason for your wait.

Yet, you protest. You say, "But my marriage is in trouble," or "I've hurt my loved ones," or "my child is rebelling, and I don't know what to do. I'm trying to get through it or past it and I can't. . . ."

What God hears is: "I hurt."

What He responds is: "I know." And then He tells you what to do with the pain. He gives you an alternative to that horrible lost feeling of abandonment and insecurity: "Be joyful in hope, patient in affliction, faithful in prayer" (Romans 12:12 NIV). There is so much to do. "Follow my lead," He says.

*Joyful in hope.* There is unparalleled joy in the pure surrender of your doubt to your Lord. Remember, part of your coffeebook writing includes giving praise to God. When you need to rediscover His guidance, it helps to remember that praise. Focus on the times that you have felt His gentle guiding hand, and let those experiences carry you now. You cannot be joyful and doubtful at the same time. It's just not possible. Which feeling do you think your Lord wants you to embrace? You can do nothing with a doubt except validate it or eliminate it. It's your choice. If you choose to eliminate it, you can replace it with joyfulness. The quickest way to do that is to give your doubts to God because He'll know what to do with them. Your joy is in trusting Him with them.

*Patient in affliction.* You already know how to do this! You're learning how to wait purposefully through the tough and trying times so that you can move closer to God and fulfill His plans for you. We know that the affliction (the wait), whether it's anger or pain or frustration, will end. Waiting for it to end means *working* to end it— surrendering to God so that we can learn more about His plans. You can't learn if you don't believe the lessons will teach you anything. You can't uncover guidance if you doubt it's there. So we can be patient enough, but we don't have to be still—it takes lots of work to overcome deep doubt. God says to do it while we wait. Our patience comes with a to-do list, and God alone decides what goes on it.

*Faithful in prayer.* Ahh, the cornerstone of our lessons! The only way to learn how to wait purposefully, to move nearer to the Lord and to uncover what we need, is to go to Him in prayer, every single day, with every single question. Your coffeebook is your guide for getting through this wait and any other, the place where you pray to God in the way that reaches Him and enlightens you. Learn how to give up your futile fight to redesign your waiting room. Surrender to the only One who knows the way out. Then grab onto the guidance you need when you think you can't see through your own impatience, and remember that God can, right to your heart.

> *I will lead the blind by ways they have not known,*
> *along unfamiliar paths I will guide them;*
> *I will turn the darkness into light before them*
> *and make the rough places smooth.*
> *These are the things I will do;*
> *I will not forsake them.*
> ISAIAH 42:16 NIV

## ⋛ *While You Wait* ⋚

- How have you neglected God's guidance in the past?

- How will you try today to surrender your doubt to Him?

- Write in your coffeebook about *today's* guidance, without doubting that tomorrow's will come on time.

# CHAPTER 21—*The Daily Steps*

If it's guidance that you seek, getting closer to God is the only way to feel it in your heart, as your thoughts become more of Him, less of you. To understand the Lord's guidance, you must be in an intimate relationship with Him, dependent and childlike, humble and open, revealing yourself in all your weakness. It's okay. Start in your waiting room: "Test me, LORD, AND TRY ME, examine my heart and my mind; for I have always been mindful of your unfailing love and have lived in reliance on your faithfulness" (Psalm 26:2–3 NIV).

"Okay, Lord, You've convinced me to surrender my doubt to You. Now, here is my life, my heart, and my hope, while I wait. I'm still afraid."

"Don't be. Believe in me—that is always where you start. Don't worry. I will prove myself in your heart if that's what you need. I am the only one who can."

> *For since the beginning of the world*
> *Men have not heard nor perceived by the ear,*
> *Nor has the eye seen any God besides You,*
> *Who acts for the one who waits for Him.*
>
> ISAIAH 64:4 NKJV

"Okay, but You know I need specifics, *work* to do while I wait and believe."

"Yes, I know."

"It seems so complicated."

"It's not. I need you to keep only these three points in mind while we work."

God is so organized.

1. Accept. "Trust in the Lord with all your heart, and lean not on your own understanding. . ." (Proverbs 3:5 NKJV). Waiting for God's guidance means being willing to accept the answers He gives, even when it appears to go against "your own understanding" Perhaps in addition to waiting for guidance, you're waiting for the wrong thing on the *outside*, too. Take the time to reexamine your external wait. Is it what you truly want, or are you just following an old pattern of behavior that is comfortable and familiar?

Sometimes, we fight the Lord's guidance because we're afraid to accept it. What if it means you've been mistaken about your wait, or your plans, or your whole life? "No problem," God says, "we start anew every day." You only have to be willing to accept His lead, to put your trust in what your heart is telling you. Decide now to accept the answers God's spirit sends to yours.

2. Acknowledge. "In all your ways acknowledge Him. . ." (Proverbs 3:6 NKJV). Open up and let God see your whole life, and more importantly, open up to yourself through your coffeebook. Acknowledge God's guidance in *every single moment* of your life. Don't let your doubts pick and choose what you give to God. Give it all to Him, ask Him anything, trust Him with everything.

> *God is not human, that he should lie,*
> *not a human being, that he should change his mind.*
> *Does he speak and then not act?*
> *Does he promise and not fulfill?*
> NUMBERS 23:19 NIV

If you try to surrender just a little bit to God, He'll know. It's like trying to carry on a conversation with someone who's preoccupied with the newspaper: most unsatisfying and practically useless. You have to start over at the beginning. That's how it is with your doubts about God. As long as you keep some of them (because He might not *really* know as much as you do about your job or your family or whatever), God doesn't have your full attention. And He won't settle for anything less than your trust and faith "in *all* your ways." The verse is not arbitrary, and your surrender can't be either.

3. Accomplish. "And He shall direct your paths" (Proverbs 3:6 NKJV). It doesn't say "show you your destination" because that's not what we need to know. We only need to travel down the paths God chooses, alongside Him and unafraid to do our work. God will never hide His guidance from you. If you don't see it and feel it in your heart, it's because you're looking too far ahead. You need only look at one step at a time and do the things He says, *one at a time.* Don't doubt your ability to do that. "Go ahead and test me," the Lord says. "Listen to me and accomplish what I put before you today. Take the step that always moves you closer to me while you wait, purposefully."

Even if circumstances are bleak and the wait grows long, we do not have to doubt when we look only to God and not to ourselves, trusting that He will hear us and make sure that we hear Him above all of the worry and fear and clutter that tries to distract us from Him.

> *But as for me, I watch in hope for the LORD,*
> *I wait for God my Savior;*
> *my God will hear me.*
> MICAH 7:7 NIV

The Lord's directions come one at a time, one step out of the wait and one step closer to Him. We don't have to know the second step to take the first, when we rediscover God's guidance and rest against His heart in the absence of doubt.

## ❧ While You Wait ❧

— In what aspects of your life is accepting God's guidance difficult for you?

— How can you turn over your external wait to God and acknowledge His lead?

— Take one step today that you fully believe is guided by God. How did it feel?

# CHAPTER 22—The Guidance, the Rest

When you begin to feel God's guiding hand and to reach to Him for your instruction every day, you will find the part of your wait that includes moving closer to Him, listening more closely to Him. And what a glorious part it is! You will find more security than you've ever known before. You will find that you can *accept, acknowledge,* and *accomplish.* But there is more. There always is.

> *"Who among you fears the LORD?*
> *Who obeys the voice of His Servant?*
> *Who walks in darkness*
> *And has no light?*
> *Let him trust in the name of the LORD*
> *And rely upon his God."*
> ISAIAH 50:10 NKJV

Learning to rediscover and follow God's guidance provides a two-fold bonus. He always gives us so much more than we give Him. You can enjoy these two gifts through and beyond your wait. They are forever yours.

## Comfort in knowing that God is in charge

I don't know about you, but I get very tired when I doubt. I grow weary of trying to carry on by myself, trying to configure everything in my life when I feel so inept to make even the tiniest decision. I get tired of waiting for changes on the outside while I curse the void on the inside. Relying on my judgment instead of seeking God's isn't comfortable at all; in fact, it's exhausting.

You'll find the same exhaustion, proven to you in a wait, as often as it takes for you to relinquish your control and lessen the grip you have on your plans and tighten the grip you have on the Lord's hand, with Him in front, leading the way. It's pure rest, needed and welcomed.

When I rely on God's guidance and trust in Him to provide it, I find comfort that comes directly from Him to me—nothing hard to understand, just a calm like no other. When I spend my waiting time getting closer to Him, my thoughts of "how can I solve this problem" are set aside, impotent. I cleave to God's direction and the infinitesimal feelings and nudges that He gives me, because I trust that each push is in the direction He needs me to go to do what He needs me to do: "I can do all things through Christ who strengthens me" (Philippians 4:13 NKJV). I can do nothing without Him.

Instead of always trying to see so far into the future that I hate waiting for, I can close my eyes and rest against God's compassion and let Him lead, knowing that even when I annoy Him, He will be there. Even when I doubt, He will be there when I manage to push the doubt away. I can wait and marvel at the comfort God gives, in good times or bad, because He must comfort me to guide me. I must take a breath and reach for Him so that He can breathe me into His arms. He is in charge. And learning that through my wait is a most wonderful comfort.

## Confidence in making decisions

That is such a promise, that I can do all things "through Him." No, it doesn't say how, and I won't hear if I doubt, but by rediscovering the Lord's guidance, I can lean upon His strength. Sometimes, we want to skip that part and just do all things that our minds tell us we should do. We want to feel confidence in our own thoughts and abilities. "Go ahead if you must," God says, "but any real confidence comes through me." There is no confidence otherwise, no rest, no peace. There is only doubt.

Still, we want God's guidance on our own terms. We want written instructions delivered to our in-box each morning so that we don't have to guess, but that's not what we get. He said that we grow our confidence *through* each wait, not after it. We learn on God's timetable, at the pace He sets for us. Every time we have to slow down and wait to grow nearer to Him to rediscover His guidance, we gain a little more confidence in our ability to hear—and that leads to confidence in the decisions we have to make. The only way to hear with your heart is to get nearer to God's. "Believe and it will be so," He says, "do not doubt."

We don't have to be like Gideon who, assured of the Lord's presence (Judges 6:12, 14, 16) and protection (Judges 6:17–23), needed even further proof of His guidance, not once, but twice more.

*Gideon said to God,*
*"If you will save Israel by my hand as you have promised—*
*look, I will place a wool fleece on the threshing floor.*
*If there is dew only on the fleece and all the ground is dry,*
*then I will know that you will save Israel by my hand, as you said."*
*And that is what happened. Gideon rose early the next day;*
*he squeezed the fleece and wrung out the dew—a bowlful of water.*
*Then Gideon said to God, "Do not be angry with me.*
*Let me make just one more request. Allow me one more test*
*with the fleece, but this time make the fleece dry and let the ground*
*be covered with dew." That night God did so. Only the fleece was dry;*

*all the ground was covered with dew.*
JUDGES 6:36–40 NIV

It's just not necessary, but it's our human nature to want validation
after validation. Show me, we say, then show me again. "Wait," God
says, "and you will see that once is forever. My guidance does not
change. . . ." Use your waiting time to discover that you don't have to
"put out the fleece" to know God's guidance.

You don't have to test God—just listen for Him. Feel His comfort
and have the confidence to trust in what you hear because He's guided
you before and I know that you've felt it and you can remember it.
Touch those feelings. Even if it was in just a small way that you let
God in and felt Him, build on that and on the confidence it inspires.
Know that the Lord's guidance will never "feel" wrong, and it will
never leave you with any doubt. Only wait for God's words to beat
into your heart.

Sooner or later, this wait will be over, the wait for the job or the
mate or the move or whatever it is on the outside, but your journey
to move nearer to God never ends because you can never get too
close. The need for His guidance just shows up in a pushier way
during times of waiting, when you feel lost and confused. When you
learn to trust and take the steps that God directs, you are working
purposefully on what He wants you to do. It may not always be what
you imagined or even what you hoped for, but if God is leading you
there, it *is* what is right.

"Lord, I want to hear You and trust You to lead me. I want to use
my waiting time to open my heart to Yours."

"Yes, you will learn how to listen while you wait, but that is only
the beginning."

"Then what?"

"You must rediscover the courage to follow my guidance."

"*Rediscover* it? I already have it, too?"

"Of course. I gave you everything you'll ever need when I spoke you to life. Do you doubt me?"

Now what could I say to that?

Rediscovering my courage sounded even harder than trusting the Lord's guidance. I'd better hope for a long wait. . . .

## ⸱ While You Wait ⸱

- What does God's comfort feel like when you hear Him?

- How can you rest in His comfort today?

- Where can you apply the confidence in God's guidance in your wait today?

- Have you ever "put out the fleece" to test God's Word?

- Write in your coffeebook about your quest to discover God's will, from His heart to yours.

_____

_____

_____

_____

_____

_____

_____

_____

_____

_____

_____

*Lord, You know how weak and resistant I can be. And yet, I crave
Your guidance through this wait and beyond. I don't want to take even
one step alone. Please open my eyes to the paths You want to show me.
Please open my ears to Your silent words of comfort and faithfulness.
Please open my heart to Yours.*

*Rediscovering God's guidance isn't about finding a treasure map—
it's about trusting the mapmaker even when you have no map.*

## PART 5

## Rediscovering the Courage That's Hidden by Fear

*For God has not given us a spirit of fear, but of power and of love and of a sound mind.*
2 TIMOTHY 1:7 NKJV

## CHAPTER 23—*Lost in the Fear*

"Why are you so afraid?" God wants to know.

"Because I feel alone, inadequate, and unsure."

"But you know that's not right, don't you?"

"Maybe, but I feel weak. I have so very little courage sometimes."

"That's not true," God said. "You have all the courage you will ever need. I've already given it to you."

"Where is it? I need it."

"You have it. You've just hidden it under your fear. It's time to rediscover it, so that we can complete this wait and do something wonderful."

I hate to admit it, to you or to God, but I was the original Cowardly Lion, afraid of what I could see and more afraid of what I couldn't see, always terrified of what would happen next in my life. God said that I didn't have to feel that way. I can't do His work if I'm afraid, so while I wait, I must work to rediscover the courage that is already mine as surely as my breath. It's not easy. But I am learning to hear God's guidance, and that leads to courage as well.

It's easy to admire those who fight fires or wars, prejudice or illness, handicap or other horrors. We stand in awe of them and wonder where they get their amazing courage. Were they born with it? I think so. But they aren't alone. Their courage was breathed into them by God's grace, but it was not limited or rationed to a chosen few. God gave the same to you and to me, too, as much as we would need. The "spirit of fear" that I carry around in my heart was not part of God's genetic plan for me. I've bred it and cultivated it and learned it all on my own. But it doesn't have to stay that way.

*The LORD is my light and my salvation; whom shall I fear?*
*The LORD is the strength of my life; of whom shall I be afraid?*
PSALM 27:1 NKJV

This "spirit of fear" isn't the life-preserving, logical fear that keeps you from surfing in a hurricane or driving with your eyes shut. It's the limiting, groundless fear that somehow takes on a life of its own, full of the trepidation and uncertainty that holds us down and prevents us from growing in our life with God and everyone here on earth. When you have to slow down and wait, you have a unique entreaty into rediscovering the courage that God planted in you from the beginning. In a wait, you will always need that courage. How lucky for you that the Lord's already given it to you!

Believe that the courage you seek is there, underneath, just as the guidance you need is there. You don't have to develop or manufacture your courage, you just have to banish the fear that's hiding it. It starts with listening for God's guidance and progresses to accepting His comfort and resting in His power.

No matter what you face or how long and difficult your wait is, it's not bigger than the sackful of courage God gave you. You just don't recognize the courage that's in you because you have that sack tied and taped and buried in the very human fear that covers it up. Let it out! It's bursting at the seams! Look at what 2 Timothy 1:7 says— *a spirit of power, love, and a sound mind.* What a gift!

Do you know why God gave you these things? It's not because He threw them into your soul like butter-bowls full of leftovers. No, He gave them to you because He knew that you needed them. He held your playbook in His hands and saw what you would need to contribute to the game. He gave these gifts to your spirit—in the exact quantities that *you* need—so that you could do the work He has for you. And in His loving father way that He cannot deny, He says that you have to get closer to Him to truly see them and draw from them. He wants you near Him, and He'll wait until you come.

The Lord may be infinitely patient with us and our problems, but He's not very lax about His own agenda. Why would He give you something to do and no gumption to do it with? It makes no sense. So rest assured that whatever work God has for you, you are equipped to handle it beautifully, guarded by angels themselves to carry it out.

> *I will say of the Lord, "He is my refuge and my fortress;*
> *My God, in Him I will trust." He shall cover you with His feathers,*
> *And under His wings you shall take refuge;*
> *His truth shall be your shield and buckler.*
> *You shall not be afraid of the terror by night,*
> *Nor of the arrow that flies by day,*
> *Nor of the pestilence that walks in darkness,*
> *Nor of the destruction that lays waste at noonday.*
> *For He shall give His angels charge over you,*
> *To keep you in all your ways.*
> PSALM 91:2, 4–6, 11 NKJV

I've thought about my own lack of courage many times, or rather, my inability to find it. I can just see God pacing up there sometimes thinking: *I've guided her here and I've told her what to do, so what is she waiting on? What's her problem? There is nothing to fear.* And yet, like a living Moses, I argue with God and try to convince Him that I'm not who He thinks I am. It is a pointless argument, and He always has the last word.

"Lord, I know You think You know what You're doing. I know You can see far beyond my limited scope, but I'm not able to go on. I have no courage, and my spirit is weak."

"I *do* know what I'm doing. And I know what *you're* doing. My Spirit in you is stronger than any spirit of fear, ever. Can you believe me?"

"I want to, Lord. Please give me the strength and courage to carry on in the face of my fears."

"Done."

## ❖ While You Wait ❖

- What do you fear most in your wait?

- How have you talked to God about your lack of courage?

- Can you believe that God has already given you all the courage you'll ever need?

# Chapter 24—The Spirit of Power

For God has not given us a spirit of fear, but of power...

The Bible tells us of many brave men and women who had courage because they believed in the power of God. That power allowed them to do powerful things as well. Do you think that they were ever afraid? I imagine that they were from time to time, in a human sort of way, but their courage was far stronger than any fear. They held onto the power of God and did their jobs. So can you.

*But he said to me, "My grace is sufficient for you,*
*for my power is made perfect in weakness."*
2 Corinthians 12:9 niv

While you wait, immerse yourself in the power of God, and allow yourself to marvel at the mind-boggling examples of it. Then feel that same power within you that He gives you to accomplish your work. It is very strong.

How can you feel that power and claim it for your own, you want to know. You start by feeling it in the little things that you do every day. God is there, and everything right that you do is powered by Him. Sometimes, it takes a spirit of power just to say you're sorry to someone. Sometimes, when you pause before you speak an unkind word and don't really know why, that is His Spirit of power working in you. While you wait, pay attention and recognize these breaths of power that God is sending you with a wink.

Slow down...wait...rediscover the power that God gave you to make good choices for Him. You can claim that Spirit of power to help you through the tiniest episodes of your life and the biggest decisions that you'll ever make. It will become another habit of fellowship with the Lord that you'll wonder how you ever lived without—and why you let the fear keep it away.

## Waiting for the power

We desperately want to cling to God's power during a wait. We want His power to adjust the timing that aggravates us so. We want His power to move the people and events that stand in our way. We want His power on our terms and our timetable, but it doesn't work that way.

God's power works *through* us on His schedule. The Spirit of power He's given us works to move us closer to Him so that we can take our next step with courage, not concern ourselves with someone else's. The spirit of power He wants us to rediscover is the Spirit that replaces the fear in our hearts with complete and unquestionable faith. When you feel the Lord's power, it's because your faith is stronger than the fear. That's what *He's* waiting for: for you to grab onto that first fleeting moment of total bravery when you relied on His power to guide and protect you, and then to turn that moment into so many more.

The bravery came when you opened your heart, maybe in the midst of a terrible wait, just long enough to rediscover His courage beneath your fear. One moment like that is all God needs for you to carry on. Then you'll open your heart a little wider and feel His power again, like a shock of courage to your struggling spirit. The more you believe in His power, the more you use it, and the more completely it banishes the draining spirit of fear. There is nothing to fear when

God Himself has provided a way for you to tap into His power.

"I don't want you to ever be afraid. Your fear stands between you and my power," the Lord explains.

"But my wait is frightening. There is so much I cannot control."

"That's because it's not your job to control the wait. It's your job to eliminate the fear that's controlling *you*."

"How?"

"Replace it with my power that I give to you. Is it so hard to believe that I would give you these things that you need?"

"No, it's just hard to rediscover them," I tell Him honestly.

"It's only hard when you make it so. It's easy when you look at me. Look while you wait."

> *Do you not know?*
> *Have you not heard?*
> *The* LORD *is the everlasting God,*
> *the Creator of the ends of the earth.*
> *He will not grow tired or weary,*
> *and his understanding no one can fathom.*
> *He gives strength to the weary*
> *and increases the power of the weak.*
>
> ISAIAH 40:28–29 NIV

When you feel weak, that's when the spirit of fear is stronger than the spirit of power. But it's always your choice which one you will hold to your heart. You don't have to be afraid that the Lord's Spirit of power will disappear or be inadequate. "My power is yours," the Lord says, "and you can never deplete it. Trust me. . . ."

## ⁍ *While You Wait* ⁌

- Where can you use the Spirit of power in your wait today?

- How will you let God's power eliminate your fear?

- Which is stronger: your spirit of fear or your spirit of power? Which is God-given?

# CHAPTER 25—*The Spirit of Love*

A spirit of love. . .

All of the work God has for you to do relies on your spirit of love that reaches to Him, to others, to yourself. Nothing that you need to do will ever go against that. Use the courage it builds to go forward with your work. In our busy worlds, sometimes full of hatred, deceit, and betrayal, the spirit of love is masked by a strong spirit of fear.

Especially in a difficult wait where we long for our own redemption, our spirit of love flounders. It feels weak and the fear of more pain and more rejection is too powerful, so we retreat. We resolve to only endure the wait that gets heavier and heavier every day because we're farther and farther away from God every day. We can't see what the wait would teach.

We feel anything but courage, and the fear lets our anger and mistrust of God and others grow. But remember, the Lord has given you the tool to rediscover your courage and use your spirit of love— and how very powerful it is! He instructs us to care for one another and to *forgive*, not just halfheartedly, but as He forgave us.

> *And over all these virtues put on love,*
> *which binds them all together in perfect unity.*
> COLOSSIANS 3:14 NIV

There is no perfect unity where lack of forgiveness exists. There is no fear where forgiveness has passed. It is the part of the Spirit of love that pushes the fear the farthest away, God's perfect love that "casts out fear" (1 John 4:18 NKJV). We can't define this Spirit of love, but we can feel its strength when we use our God-given tools. You can choose either a spirit of fear or a spirit of love, but not both.

"Don't ever be afraid to forgive," God says. "It will uncover more courage than you know."

"Courage to get me through my wait?"

"Courage to get you through your entire *life*, so that you can do all you ever need to do, without fear."

Fear is a human emotion. Courage is a spiritual gift. It's your gift from God, and you rediscover it when you dispel what's hiding it and unleash its power. The fear supported by a lack of forgiveness is no match for the Spirit of love applied with God-force through you.

> *Let all that you do be done with love.*
> 1 CORINTHIANS 16:14 NKJV

## ⋅ *While You Wait* ⋅

- How have you let fear keep you from granting forgiveness to yourself or others?

- Where in your life is the spirit of love weak or faltering?

- Find one place in your wait today to replace a fear with God's Spirit of love.

# CHAPTER 26—*The Spirit of a Sound Mind*

Of a sound mind. . .

Feeling the power of God and the love of God works in conjunction with the mind of God. Some translations use the word "self-discipline" in this verse. The spirit of a sound mind/self-discipline is part of the generous gifts God's given you so that you need not be afraid. He wants us to be bold and courageous, and He promises an answer to our very real human fears that expand and gain momentum when we have to wait:

> *When you pass through the waters,*
> *I will be with you;*
> *And through the rivers,*
> *they shall not overflow you.*
> *When you walk through the fire,*
> *you shall not be burned.*
> ISAIAH 43:2 NKJV

Sometimes, we're afraid of failing. Sometimes, we believe that we just can't get where we want to be because we're not strong enough or smart enough or courageous enough. If you ever feel that way, you're wrong, and you can understand how you're wrong if you will only think it out logically, with a "sound mind." Think yourself through your wait by applying God's guidance to the work you do every day, the best way you know how.

God says to wait purposefully—not in fear of the outcome or your own inadequacies, but with the spirit of a sound mind that listens and learns best while in your waiting room. If you trust in and claim God's Spirit of power for your own and wrap it in a spirit of love, then you can step over the fear with the spirit of a sound mind that makes clear to you what is *right* for you. And when you know, you can't be afraid. God's given His Spirit to you, and when it's alive in your soul (His power) and your heart (His love) and your mind (His discipline), there is no room for a spirit of fear.

Where you need to be is wherever God leads you. And if you find yourself afraid and in a place where God did not lead you, then He will show you the courage to find a better place while you wait. The spirit of fear will try to overtake all of your senses, but God's Spirit is bigger than that. It will sustain you and encourage you and hold you up when you think you'll fall. Trust it. Pray it into your heart.

God's Spirit is never more alive than in moments of prayer. Go to Him, write to Him, and listen for the answers that will turn away the fear. He will speak to your mind so that you won't be afraid to do the work He has for you—and it is uniquely your work as surely as the tree grows its only fruit: "But blessed is the one who trusts in the LORD, whose confidence is in him. They will be like a tree planted by the water that sends out its roots by the stream. It does not fear when heat comes; its leaves are always green. It has no worries in a year of drought and never fails to bear fruit" (Jeremiah 17:7–8 NIV).

## ⋛ While You Wait ⋚

- How has your "sound mind" given way to the fear of your wait?

- In what one way can you apply the spirit of self-discipline to your wait today?

- Write to God about your spirit of a sound mind and listen for His direction.

## CHAPTER 27—Banishing the Spirit of Fear

How will you know when you have banished your spirit of fear? Maybe when your wait is over? That's possible, but it can be a fleeting comfort, and the spirit of fear is strong and relentless. It wants to hold you back and keep you away from your Lord. You will know you've banished your spirit of fear when you feel it getting weaker and weaker, in these two ways, through your wait and beyond.

*Your attitude.* If you wait purposefully in search of the Lord's guidance and companionship, you will think of yourself in a new way—courageous and strong. Your "spirit of power, love and a sound mind" will become more and more accessible to you. You will not think: "What if I fail?" You will only hear in your heart: "How will God help me with this?" You will have an attitude of bravery that will never fail you.

*"Fear not. . .for I am your God.*
*I will strengthen you,*
*Yes, I will help you,*
*I will uphold you with My righteous right hand."*
Isaiah 41:10 NKJV

*Your actions.* You will do your work with trust, without fear, every day as God directs, learning while you wait. You'll know what your work is because the Lord led you to it, and you will have the courage to carry it out with His Spirit alive in you. Each step you take will reinforce your attitude of courage, which will then lead you to another step. He's already given you all the courage you need for every part of your journey. The trust in its power is yours to grow.

When you rediscover your courage, use all you want. You have a never-ending supply.

Our courage isn't about knowing what will happen in the far distant future—that's like having psychic abilities or a crystal ball that actually works. Courage is going on even when you don't know everything, simply trusting God to lead you in the right direction one step at a time. Is it a blind guess? No, it's confidence in God's guidance and rest in His Spirit. You rediscover your real courage in the face of fear, and then a funny thing happens: the fear goes away.

## A vision revisited

I sometimes like to recall a "vision" I used to have many years ago. It wasn't a daydream or a night dream. It was just a scene in my mind that came to me when I needed it most.

During a very painful wait and frightening period of my life, I would lie in bed and pray, but only in my mind because I was too lost to even form the words. I felt devoid of any strength or courage as well as the hope of rediscovering any that I'd ever had. But then, the vision began to come.

Each night, as I was still and quiet after I had wiped away a year's worth of tears, I would see myself walking across a tightrope, one shaky step in front of the other. And then I would look down and there, right under the rope, was the huge hand of God, His palm open and soft, ready to catch me gently if I should fall. There were no words, just the recurring vision that stilled my pain for a moment and gave way to rest. I would finally go to sleep with that vision in my heart, a comfort like no other.

When the fear you face in your wait is almost tangible, banish it with the comfort of God's courage that He longs to share with you. You are not alone, because the Lord is waiting under your tightrope, too. Maybe it's stretched across your waiting room, His hand soft and safe underneath. Look and see.

"Will you let the fear go away now?" He asks.

"I want to. I want to feel Your courage and keep the frightening feelings far away. They are so unsettling."

"You have something for that, too, you know—my peace that I breathed into you at the start."

"At the start of my wait?"

"At the start of your life. It's there, waiting for you to rediscover it, too."

"You'll show me how, while we wait?"

"Of course. Surely, you can't be afraid. . . ."

There He went again, leading me farther and farther out of my waiting room and closer and closer to Him. *Thank You, Lord.*

### ❧ While You Wait ❧

- How can you replace a fearful attitude with a courageous attitude today?

- What courageous actions have you been afraid to take?

- Put yourself in the "tightrope" vision. What do you see underneath? How will you rediscover the courage to make it across?

................................................................................

................................................................................

Lord, it seems so much easier to be afraid than courageous, and yet, You know my spirit longs for the courage that only You supply. Show me the power that You have designed to fight the fear. Show me the love that is stronger than the past. Show me the self-discipline that helps me stay the course. Show me the courage You've already given me for this wait. Show me my fear—the weak and groundless fear that vanishes with Your touch. Then show me the wonders that appear in its wake.

Courage is the path on which your work travels.
Fear is just a pothole that you fill with faith.

## PART 6

## Rediscovering the Peace
## That's Hidden by Worry

*Be anxious for nothing, but in everything by prayer and supplication,*
*with thanksgiving, let your requests be made known to God;*
*and the peace of God, which surpasses all understanding,*
*will guard your hearts and minds through Christ Jesus.*
PHILIPPIANS 4:6–7 NKJV

CHAPTER 28—*Misplacing God's Peace*

"You seem restless," God says. "Why are you struggling so?"

"I'm worried about so many things, and I wonder if I will ever feel the peace that You say is mine, that You say I already have."

"Yes, my peace is with you, but you can't feel it unless you come into my arms. The path you take to rediscover it is through your worry. Don't be afraid."

"But my worry is thick and dense. I don't know *how* to go through it."

"By believing it isn't there."

Well, could You be a little more vague, Lord? There I was, so insecure in my wait, and God gave me a riddle. I didn't see how I could get through my worry and reach the other side, but I had learned not to be afraid of the journey or doubt the Lord's direction. I desperately needed to feel His peace as well, in my waiting room or not, and yet it seemed foreign to me. Why couldn't I believe and trust and feel the peace that God had granted? Where was the peace I had misplaced? It had to be there, God said so. It had to still be mine, because God said our work wasn't done, and I could not do His work without His peace. So I knew it must still be there, waiting, masked by the worries that He would help me scatter like stones into a canyon, lost in the depth of something much bigger. Your peace is still there, too, even if you don't see it right now.

*We are hard pressed on every side, but not crushed;*
*perplexed, but not in despair;*
*persecuted, but not abandoned;*
*struck down, but not destroyed.*
2 CORINTHIANS 4:8–9 NIV

## The peace of this life

Have you ever watched a young child sleep? I used to look at my son when he was three or four and marvel at the look of pure peace on his sleeping face. What was more amazing was that he looked pretty much the same when he was awake. He felt great peace in his everyday life, complete confidence that I would be there to take care of him, that he would be fed, warm, and safe. He was at peace with his world, albeit a very sheltered one. But he's a teenager now, and sometimes I see the look of worry on his face. His world is not as peaceful as it once was, and there are traces of concern and uncertainty that spill onto the tranquility he once knew. We are all that way.

We grow up into a world that can be anything but peaceful, and none of us can ever reclaim that unique kind of peace that a young child has, that never-threatened security of a life barely lived. We can't reclaim it because that kind of peace is based on a never-tested faith. Adulthood brings faith tested all too often! Adulthood brings waiting times that threaten everything we've ever learned or believed in. The waiting can unsettle the peace we thought we'd claimed as our own. But it doesn't have to be that way. The serenity is possible again, just in a different way.

> *"These things I have spoken to you, that in Me you may have peace.*
> *In the world you will have tribulation; but be of good cheer,*
> *I have overcome the world."*
> JOHN 16:33 NKJV

As grown-ups, we can have and hold something even better than a child's peace. We can have a peace based on a full knowledge of the Lord and His promises, on a faith that has been tested and yet survived, on a unique, one-on-one relationship with God.

When we have to wait, that comfort and peace can seem to disappear, like the light of a candle extinguished by the force of an angry shout. We lose our way, and God provides the guidance. We lose our courage, and God gives us strength. Yet we cling to our worry because the world we live in creates it anew each morning. Each day, we have to fight the world and ourselves to get to what we so desperately want and can't see—the Lord's peace that has lived in us from the very beginning. The human side of us is struggling, the spirit is in need of renewal. "That's okay," God says, "now's the time."

What is it about waiting that makes us worry so? It's the same thing that allows us to deepen our relationship with God: *time.* The more time passes in our wait, the more we worry because we question everything all over again. The more time passes as we wait purposefully with God, the closer we get to Him. Over time, we worry, or over time, we learn and grow. The time will pass either way.

It's when we fail to trust in God's control of our time that the worry grows, planted like a forest between Him and us, a forest that grows thick and fast and tall. And yet it can be crossed with one step in the right direction.

"Don't you want to rediscover your peace?" the Lord asks.

"Of course, but I feel like my wait will never end. It's blinding in its pain."

"What do you see?"

"My worries, big and scary."

"That's because you're looking at them from over there. From here, they are flat and tame." Even His words sound calm and safe.

"How can I see them that way?"

"Step over here."

Sometimes it's hard to take that step and believe that God knows best, even when we see our part of the plan and feel the courage to participate in it. Time passes slowly and shifts your focus. You forget how far you've come and how much you've grown. When the world says that you're wrong to claim God's peace and you don't feel His answers in your heart, it's easy to fall back on the worries that put you in your waiting room in the first place. You wonder if the peace you crave will ever be truly yours. You needn't worry. It already is. Use your waiting time to rediscover it.

*And my God will meet all your needs*
*according to the riches of his glory in Christ Jesus.*
PHILIPPIANS 4:19 NIV

## ❧ *While You Wait* ❧

- How has your wait hidden God's peace from you?

- Where do you need to feel God's peace instead of the world's control?

- What step will you take today to fill your waiting time with more peace and less worry?

# CHAPTER 29—*Rediscovering God's Peace*

So where is this elusive peace you want? It's hidden underneath the worry, because you cannot be peaceful and worried at the same time. It won't work. One of the two emotions will win out. That's the way it is for everything God's already given you. It's your choice which you will embrace and claim as your own: guidance or doubt, courage or fear, and yes, peace or worry. Which one do you think God needs you to feel to do your work?

While you wait, you can search His heart and rest in His promises. We don't have to live with a broken heart and a troubled mind because if we believe, "This is how we know that we belong to the truth and how we set our hearts at rest in his presence: If our hearts condemn us, we know that God is greater than our hearts, and he knows everything" (1 John 3:19–20 NIV).

"If you want to feel peace, you must breathe it in and breathe out the worry. Breathe in my promises, breathe in my love, breathe in my compassion. Breathe out the anger, breathe out the mistrust, breathe out the busyness that keeps you from me."

"Lord, please show me how."

"Have I ever not shown you what you needed to know? Trust me and rediscover the peace you want. I need you to trust me."

"But my faith is weak. How can I trust when I feel so unsure?"

"Look inside your heart. To feel my peace, you must trust that I will help you to rediscover it. To find it, you must believe that it's *already there.* Start now."

The promise was too great to let it pass. I had to try.

"Okay, step one. I can do this?"

"With my help, you can. We're in this together, remember?"

"I do so want to wake up in Your peace."

"You can. I never sleep, you know. . . ."

I just love it when He points out the obvious. God told me to find
comfort in our conversations. The words that we shared were part
of the purpose, part of learning my place in His plan. He challenged
me to look back at the times that I had been wrong to worry when
I waited. He dared me to think that He had ever led me in the wrong
way or that His answers had ever come at the wrong time. No matter
what I had waited for, God was there with me, trying to get me to rest
in His peace. I fought it and doubted it many times, but that didn't change
the fact that it was always there. I can see that now as I look back.

I can see how I resisted the peace He wanted to give me because I
thought I knew better. I professed to want His guidance and courage
and peace, but instead, I wanted His agreement and answers and
applause for handling something by myself. When I did refuse His
help and handle something without Him to the best of my inability,
the feeling that followed was not what I had hoped for. My efforts
never brought even the hint of the kind of peace I craved so. I was
running such a con on myself in the belief that I was responsible for
manufacturing my peace.

All the while, the peace and everything else that I needed most
were already there, hidden by my own insecurity masquerading as
control, and it was in my times of waiting that I uncovered these gifts.

I know that your wait feels heavy right now, and I know it hurts.
I know what it's like to be desperate for even a fleeting moment of
peace amid the pain. I know what it's like to need someone to say
you'll be okay. And I know that there is a guaranteed instant way
to feel God's peace while you wait. Right now, write to Him in your
coffeebook, and pray just one word: *here.*

Here is where I am, now, needing Your peace.

Here is where I stand still, waiting for You to help me.

Here is where I start to discover the purpose for my wait.

Here is where I worry no more, at least for this moment.

Here is my empty heart, given to You, Lord, to fill with peace.

Be *here*. Be at peace. Then tomorrow, write to God some more, and fill your heart full again. Every day, listen when God talks to you so that you can walk through your worry together. As you learn who you are, you will find that you are first a child of God—a child held in peace, a child loved and wanted and never, ever abandoned by the one in charge of all.

*"Who has preceded Me, that I should pay him?*
*Everything under heaven is Mine."*
JOB 41:11 NKJV

## ⇒ While You Wait ⇐

- What is one step that you can take in your journey to rediscover God's peace? Write it in your coffeebook.

- What must you breathe out to breathe in God's peace? Make a list and cross the items off one by one.

## Chapter 30—*Understanding God's Peace*

❧❧❧

"I wish you wouldn't resist my peace so strongly. It isn't hard to understand," the Lord tells me.

"Yes, I know You say that I already have it, and I'm trying, but the journey to rediscover it looks long and treacherous."

"Don't you see the guiding signs?"

"There are *signs?* Where?" Was He trying to trick me?

God smiled.

"In your waiting room."

He got me again.

## *Be anxious for nothing. . .*

❧❧❧

How can you "be anxious for nothing" in the midst of a terrible wait for something that you so desperately need, when the time crawls, and still, your answers do not come? You can "be anxious for nothing" in even the most difficult wait because God gives you an alternative to the worry. "Give it to me," He says.

> *. . .but in everything by prayer and supplication, with thanksgiving, let your requests be made known to God. . .*
> PHILIPPIANS 4:6 NKJV

How much plainer can He get? "Everything" means all of the wait. Isn't that the habit you're cultivating in your coffeebook, writing about everything that troubles you, by prayer and supplication (or request), thanking and praising God for His wonderful blessings, pouring out *everything* that fills your heart? That's what your coffeebook time is for, the quiet just between you and God.

Everything in my coffeebook is big. There are family concerns and work pressures and personal issues. I might not ask how, but *why*, would God want to concern Himself with all of that and bring a restful peace to my belligerent soul. Would He stay in my waiting room with me long enough to breathe that peace of His world onto mine? The answer is yes, always, forever, no matter how much "everything" there is, or how ugly or messy it is, or how long I've kept it away from Him. He wants it all, and I'll have no peace until I give it to Him.

> *"Peace I leave with you, My peace I give to you;*
> *not as the world gives do I give to you.*
> *Let not your heart be troubled,*
> *neither let it be afraid."*
> JOHN 14:27 NKJV

If I let myself question the Lord's devotion, it's because the world is closer to my heart than He is. It's because my very human thoughts and reasons have made me question that which I cannot see or touch. But there's more than just God urging me to give Him my worries. There is a promise as well.

> *. . .and the peace of God, which surpasses all understanding,*
> *will guard your hearts and minds through Christ Jesus.*
> PHILIPPIANS 4:7 NKJV

Well, that's pretty clear, even to *me!* How beautiful—a promise of "the peace of God" to you and me. I want that! I want the "peace of God" to guard my heart and my mind, my heart and mind that are battered and beaten by the world and my wait. God's peace is like the sun. I can't see it all the time and so I think it's faded away, but it never moves. When I can't see His peace, my worry is in the way, obscuring it like a cloud. God says that I can replace that worry with my purposeful work—just give Him everything. I can will the cloud away and bask in the deepest peace that is within me always. Even when I've moved away, it's been there like a ray of light to lead me back, over the mess, closer to the Lord.

> *For God is not a God of disorder but of peace.*
> 1 CORINTHIANS 14:33 NIV

## ⸙ While You Wait ⸙

- What about this wait makes you anxious?

- How will you trust God with your worry?

- How far away is "the peace of God" from you right now? Start today to move your clouds of worry out of the way.

..................................................................................................
..................................................................................................
..................................................................................................
..................................................................................................

# CHAPTER 31—Peace Through the Wait

*Then they said to Him, "What shall we do,*
*that we may work the works of God?"*
*Jesus answered and said to them,*
*"This is the work of God,*
*that you believe in Him whom He sent."*
JOHN 6:28–29 NKJV

"Can you wait purposefully now to rediscover my peace that you want and need?" God asks.

"I could feel plenty of peace if my wait would end!" I offer, wondering why I even try.

"That's not the point," He says. "I want you to rediscover the peace that will carry you through your wait, and trust it to carry you where I lead."

"Why *this* way?" I protest.

"Because your wait will end, and then you'll begin to worry again that I'm not enough, or you'll hang the temporary peace you feel on the outcome of your wait, and you'll still be apart from me."

"But how do I rediscover Your peace *through* my wait?"

"Forget the wait," God said.

Well, clearly, He had missed the point. Or maybe I misunderstood. . . .

"Could You repeat that?"

"You heard me. Forget the wait. Forget it in the way that you change your focus from the wait to me. Focus only on *me*. The wait will end when it's time. Forget it for now and in everything, come to me."

I was having a hard time following His line of thinking there.

"My wait isn't important?"

"Of course, it's important, but it will end. The peace you need is more important, and it won't. You cannot do my work without feeling my peace, because all the guidance and courage in the world is tentative unless you rediscover my peace within you. I need you to understand and cling to that peace. That's where I am, and we have much to do."

God was right about one thing: forgetting my wait was certainly going to be work—no time to be patient when He'd given me such a purpose. My waiting room felt like it was full of pink-and-green giraffes, and God had just told me to think about anything *but* pink-and-green giraffes. My wait was the biggest thing on my mind, and He said to let it go and make Him the biggest thing on my mind, while the pain of my wait stood all around me, dwarfing me in the shadow of pink and green spots. He was right, of course, but I wondered how I'd ever learn.

So I wrote to Him. I asked Him to help me hear His guidance and have the courage to follow. I asked myself if I thought I could get through this wait *without* God's peace, and I laughed at my own question. The answer was becoming clearer, and what had seemed so complicated became quite simple. I had to make only one choice: be anxious for everything or be anxious for nothing, give the Lord everything or give Him nothing. There was no middle ground. God's grace was all that could lighten my heavy heart.

The world and the wait that I could see were out of my control. My path and my steps were in my control. What I could touch was powerless when I tried to chart my course myself. What I could feel was priceless when I reclaimed God's peace and started there.

Again, that one step is enough to open your heart to rediscovering God's peace *through* your wait, through everything that hurts. He's right by your side.

*Your word is a lamp for my feet*
*and a light on my path.*
PSALM 119:105 NIV

### ❧ *While You Wait* ❧

- How can you forget your wait and refocus your attention on God?

- Write down how you feel when you put your worries about the wait aside, even if only for a little while. How does that help you to rediscover God's peace?

# Chapter 32—*Again, the Amazing Benefits*

Every blessing that the Lord breathes our way is overflowing with His grace. It will surround you like summer from every direction and feel warm upon your heart. Your wait will become less of an *event* in your life and more of the *journey* of your life as you keep moving closer and closer to God. Past, present, and future come together to reveal to you His surrounding peace that sustains you through it all. You can recognize it so well from your waiting room, when you have chosen to give the worry to God. Then you can see those "unseen eternal things" and reap the amazing benefits of God's peace given to you, from the beginning, without end.

## Release from the past

A wait is a perfect time to let go of the past. If you are holding onto some transgression of the past and it's blocking God's peace from your heart, let God move it out of the way. Use your courage to reach out to God and "love much" as the woman who sinned and yet believed (Luke 7:36–50). God's peace is already there, so much so that you never have to worry about the past again. While you wait, purposefully release the past because the best is yet to come. Have just a little faith, and the Lord believes in you. Then you can claim this blessing for your own: "Then He said to the woman, 'Your faith has saved you. Go in peace'" (Luke 7:50 NKJV).

# Faith in the future

The faraway future may be unclear, but the one-day-at-a-time future is all you need to see. And the peace today that carries you to tomorrow will be the peace tomorrow that carries you to the next day. You do not have to worry about the future of your wait because God has already included that in His "everything." Your faith grows stronger with every heartbeat when you rest in God's peace that fills every moment like the blood in your veins. There is room for nothing else, and yet it's all you need.

> *In peace I will lie down and sleep,*
> *for you alone, LORD,*
> *make me dwell in safety.*
> PSALM 4:8 NIV

# Appreciation of the present

Rediscovering and feeling God's enormous peace fills each day to the top. "Focus on me," He said. And when you do, the days spent in your waiting are filled with more work, less worry. No matter how difficult or painful your wait is, it isn't bigger than God's plans for today. That feeling of hope, however small, is His way of telling you to appreciate and value this day, not to misuse it with worry over a wait.

We fail to recognize the unique blessing that every single day is because it dissolves in a blink. We take the days for granted and complain when they don't bring an end to our wait. But when you change your focus and you trust that God is in charge of this day, you see it for the priceless gift it is. It becomes full of potential and purpose, wrapped in God's peace, ready for you. Your faith makes it count.

*And whatever you do, whether in word or deed,*
*do it all in the name of the Lord Jesus,*
*giving thanks to God the Father through him.*
COLOSSIANS 3:17 NIV

## ⟫ While You Wait ⟪

- To what part of your past do you need to apply God's peace?

- How does your future look different when you consider it guarded by God's peace?

- Appreciate today by filling it with more work and less worry. Write to God about how you waited purposefully by appreciating today.

......................................................................................

......................................................................................

......................................................................................

......................................................................................

......................................................................................

......................................................................................

......................................................................................

......................................................................................

......................................................................................

......................................................................................

......................................................................................

......................................................................................

*My worry is so strong sometimes, Lord. It overtakes me and hides the peace You've given me. Please help me rediscover Your peace and shed my worries about the past I cannot change. Please help me rediscover Your peace that grants me faith in a future I cannot see. Please help me rediscover Your peace to learn and grow through my wait by changing my focus to rest on You, today and every day.*

*The Lord's peace is so much bigger than your worry—
you only need choose the one that will fill your heart the most.*

## PART 7

# When the Waiting Is Over

*Unless the LORD had given me help,*
*I would soon have dwelt in the silence of death.*
*When I said, "My foot is slipping,"*
*your unfailing love, LORD, supported me. . .*
*your consolation brought me joy.*
PSALM 94:17–19 NIV

# CHAPTER 33—Discovering the Purpose

"Are you happy now? Your wait is over," God says, smiling at me.

"I'm happy now," I tell Him, but I wonder if He knows why.

When the outside wait is over, we feel enormous relief. Whether the wait ended how we wanted it to or not, it feels so good to be through it. It feels as if we can breathe again and plan again, and if we're not careful, we'll try to take control again. That's the biggest threat that the end of a wait brings, the deepest hole that hides to engulf your progress on your most important journey.

We have to be careful that hindsight of a wait doesn't mistakenly show us a pain that we endured alone. Instead, we need an accurate accounting of the discovery that we shared with the Lord. If we begin to see the wait as only an outside step in our mortal lives, we'll obscure its real and spiritual purpose. We'll miss the part where we give it to God, learning to trust that He has a use for it far beyond anything we can see. Our job is first and always to *wait purposefully*.

We don't want to forget that what we worked and waited for was the growth God needed us to have—however much that was, in whatever direction He planned, regardless of what happened on the outside. And the quest for your own growth and fellowship is indeed a most glorious purpose. Only by getting near enough to God can you hear Him, so that you can take the lessons of this wait to another.

"I hope that you will trust now that your waiting room is for your benefit. It's not to annoy you, but to strengthen you. I'm always here, in your waiting room—I built it for you."

"I know that now. I've thought so often that I was here alone. I've wasted so much time."

"Nothing is wasted. I was just waiting."

If you've waited purposefully, you've made a powerful and liberating discovery: how the wait ended wasn't as important as what happened in your heart during the wait. What you began with only one step out of your waiting room was a journey that carries you where the Lord leads, one step of faith that traverses miles and miles of doubt, fear, and worry. God's view is so much clearer than ours—of our wait, of His plan, of the real purpose. You need only see as far as God, and He's right there beside you, always leading. Then you follow.

Maybe you needed to rediscover the Lord's guidance during this wait. Maybe it was courage you needed to resurrect from your fear. Maybe you desperately needed to reconnect with the peace that God alone gives. Or maybe it was something else that only God could reveal to you, something that you could find solely by moving closer to Him.

No matter what you needed, it was there all along because He knew you'd need it, so He gave it to you, along with your heart, so that your heart and your gifts from Him would be forever linked.

Even when we try to hide the gifts He's given us, we can't, because every heartbeat squeezes them out from under the pain so that we can reclaim them in an instant, completely and without fail. Our waiting time feels heavy and draining, but it is worthy and nourishing because we are connected to God by an unseen Spirit that funnels everything we need our way. He knows our souls like the wind knows the waves. How can you ever doubt your Lord's power?

*Who has measured the waters in the hollow of His hand,*
*Measured heaven with a span*
*And calculated the dust of the earth in a measure?*
*Weighed the mountains in scales*
*And the hills in a balance?*
*Who has directed the Spirit of the* Lord,
*Or as His counselor has taught Him?*
*With whom did He take counsel, and who instructed Him,*
*And taught Him in the path of justice?*
*Who taught Him knowledge,*
*And showed Him the way of understanding?*

Isaiah 40:12–14 NKJV

## ⧉ After the Wait ⧉

- What have you rediscovered through your wait?

- Write about how much closer to the Lord you feel now.

- How will you move even closer?

# Chapter 34—When You Have to Wait Again

Getting through the wait that brought you here is just another step in your journey with God. It is an experience that you and He share together, as you rediscover the wonderful blessings He's given you. Your wait is about learning how to use those gifts for yourself and for the work He has planned for you. Waiting purposefully reveals the gifts. Each wait challenges you all over again to reveal another, the one that you need the most, *at that time.*

Still, we live a constantly new beginning every day, because we easily fall back into familiar habits when our lives come to an ill-timed halt. We get frustrated with our waits because of the earthly demands on us and our own stubborn (yet futile) attempts to conform God to our timetables. It's hard to wait purposefully sometimes, no matter how much we learn in our waiting rooms, because we view the waits as external wells that we can't seem to climb out of no matter what we do. We fight the waiting time, spent and exhausted from the struggle.

Never frustrated, God is just there, no matter where we turn. "Hey, slow down, this is my time, too, and it has a purpose. Let's renew your spirit. I'll show you how," He says.

As aggravating and resistant as we are, He never gives up. He will be there in your next wait, and He will meet you wherever you are. If you've fallen back to a place that is filled with doubt and mistrust and questions, He will start there. If your faith is strong but your courage is weak, He'll work with that. There is no place where He won't be, no need He won't meet, no wait He can't use.

*The human spirit is the lamp of the Lord*
*that sheds light on one's inmost being.*
Proverbs 20:27 niv

So when your next wait comes, and it most surely will at what appears to be the most inconvenient time, remember to look for what you're lacking on the inside, in your spirit. Use your time to find it by starting *where* you are and discovering more of *who* you are every day. You don't have to concern yourself with the clock because the Lord is never late. Yet I know very well that sometimes His purposes feel very much like delays to us!

Limited by our own imperfections, we struggle along without benefit of His wisdom and never-failing strength. We stumble and fall, but *it doesn't matter* to God. He doesn't judge us as a cause lost to our absence of patience, because He knows that our human preoccupation with haste is just that—a human habit that we can bend and form to become a little more like Him through every wait. The very best time to get us to understand that opportunity is during a wait, when we *have* to push the pause button and take a breath to look at the world we're creating with every second of our time.

We spend our mortal lives on the things we wait for that are on the *outside.* Through the waiting, we save our spiritual lives with the things we rediscover on the *inside.* God challenges us to walk closely with Him and find the purpose, however long it takes. We can give up the quest for slippery, hard-to-find patience during those times, but we cannot become idle. God's work calls for our commitment and our hope, our attention and our trust, all in full, holding nothing back. And there is no time to be patient with that work! The discoveries await.

*And let us not grow weary while doing good,*
*for in due season we shall reap if we do not lose heart.*
GALATIANS 6:9 NKJV

# Unexpected help for your wait

Every now and then, in the middle of a difficult wait, you'll find a surprise. Like a dollar on the sidewalk, it may not appear to be much, and the person who dropped it will never notice, but you'll pick it up anyway and stick it in your pocket. The dollar looks the same as all the rest, but it's different. You'll remember when and where you found it. And it might just be something you'll need later on.

There was a wonderful lady that I worked with many years ago. A bit older than I, we were only acquaintances in the small company, but I always silently admired her strength and unwavering faith. One day, she "dropped a dollar," and I took it. This happened back when oil reserves and rain forest depletion were front-page news every day. Man's destruction of the planet was on everyone's mind.

A group of us were talking about the dismal forecast, and she dismissed the most vocal alarmist with a wave of her hand and a faith I wanted for my own.

"God's still in charge," she said, tossing her head the way she often did, always pretty confident about everything she said.

This woman was not an ostrich, hiding her head so that the problems wouldn't exist. She recognized the destruction that civilization brings and the challenges that we all must face, but her view of the situation was through the eyes of faith and trust, humility and belief in a God that she knew was in charge. She had rediscovered the guidance, courage, and peace she needed to frame every day of her life.

I took her comment and tucked it away in my heart. And through the years, I've never forgotten where I found it. I hear her words from time to time when I need them most, and I do my best to pass them on to others.

*As each one has received a gift, minister it to one another,*
*as good stewards of the manifold grace of God.*
1 PETER 4:10 NKJV

Our waiting room is not some kind of spiritual mousetrap that God disguises with a trick. It's a classroom, not a dungeon. Remember to carry your coffeebook to your next wait. Take notes, study, learn. Another wait is guaranteed. God's help is guaranteed. Use them both.

## ⸙ After the Wait ⸙

- What familiar habits did you have to deal with and overcome in this wait?

- Recall when someone "dropped a dollar" that benefited you. How can you pass it on to others?

........................................................................................
........................................................................................
........................................................................................
........................................................................................
........................................................................................
........................................................................................
........................................................................................
........................................................................................

# CHAPTER 35—*Helping Others Wait*

*Blessed be the God and Father of our Lord Jesus Christ,*
*the Father or mercies and God of all comfort,*
*who comforts us in all our tribulation,*
*that we may be able to comfort those who are in any trouble,*
*with the comfort with which we ourselves are comforted by God.*
2 CORINTHIANS 1:3–4 NKJV

One of the most wonderful by-products of learning to wait purposefully is your ability to share the art with others. The glorious changes that your Lord has brought about on the inside of you will escape through your skin and show themselves to others, if you will only let them.

Because we are always surrounded by waiting, there are always opportunities to be one of those souls who reaches out to another, to offer understanding, light, and love. Just as you have been ministered to by those around you, as you share in others' waits, extend to them the same God-inspired help that you've received, and delight in doing so because it is uniquely yours to give. So, "Do not withhold good from those to whom it is due, when it is in your power to act" (Proverbs 3:27 NIV). There are amazing gifts that you can share:

*Compassion.* No one knows how to share the pain of another better than someone who's been there. Your understanding of a friend's anguish is real—that makes your compassion honest, sincere, and very much appreciated.

*Camaraderie.* It can be hard for someone to travel through her wait when she's hurting and trying to find the purpose. You can walk with her, listen without judgment, and make her journey easier.

*Conviction.* When you've learned to wait purposefully, you'll inspire those around you with your renewed spirit and strength. With every breath, you'll be an example of one who has grown nearer to the Lord. And nothing will be able to shake your vision and your faith.

And God said. . .

> *Wait on the LORD;*
> *Be of good courage,*
> *And He shall strengthen your heart;*
> *Wait, I say, on the LORD!*
> PSALM 27:14 NKJV

"Do You know why I'm happy that this outside wait is over, Lord?" I ask.

"Yes, but you tell me anyway."

He *still* won't let me get a step ahead. . .thank goodness!

"I'm happy because I found out how relative it was to everything else."

"And how relative was it?"

"Not very. Everything else—listening to You, talking to You, rediscovering what I was so sure I'd lost, resting in Your heart while I was hurt and afraid—all of that became my focus, strong and clear."

"As it should be."

"This trip to my waiting room gave me a blessed perspective on Your plan. I'm happy because I know that I don't have to dread a wait ever again—I only have to wait purposefully."

"I'm happy, too. Do you want to know why?" He asks.

"I want to know everything!"

"I'm happy because you are closer to me now than when the wait began. You see, my arms and my heart can reach you wherever you are, but the closer you come, the tighter I can hold you."

"That's what I want."

"Come closer still. I'm waiting. . . ."

*Lord, I came into this wait lost, afraid, and insecure and, worst of all, distant from You. Yet You didn't leave me here alone. You were always there at the end of my prayer, waiting to catch me, hold me, teach me, grow me. I know that every wait serves only one real purpose, to move me closer to You. Please help me to always wait purposefully, because I can never be patient for the next step that draws me nearer to You. I can't wait.*

### The End

## About the Author

Karon Phillips of Alabama is an inspiration to the tens of thousands of women who've read her books *You're Late Again, Lord!*, *Grab a Broom, Lord...* and *You Still Here, Lord?* She has also written for many magazines, including *Woman's Day* and *Writer's Digest*.